PRAISE FOR THIS BOOK

"**A great resource**… As an office managing partner, I found myself saying over and over again, '_____ would really benefit from this chapter.'"

– William A. Nolan, Managing Partner, Columbus Office, Barnes & Thornburg

"Jim's book is a true testament to the changing legal landscape supported by numerous case studies and facts representative of firms in various stages of their LPM maturity. For an industry historically known for asking, 'What is everyone else doing?' this book answers that question and **ignites a sense of urgency** for lawyers and law firms to pay attention to the drum beat of the cultural transformation taking place within the legal industry. To ignore the advice and advances laid out in this book regarding LPM and pricing would be a significant oversight by the reader."

– Kim Craig, Director of Legal Project Management Office, Seyfarth Shaw LLP

"**Practical and well-balanced**… every lawyer could find valuable tools and tips in this book."

– Caroline Ferguson, Advisor (Digital and Business Improvement), Allen & Overy LLP

"The case studies helped shape our plan for developing project management skills throughout the firm. Not only were they **helpful in gaining buy-in** from management and participants, they gave a balanced perspective on how the process can (and should) be tailored to each individual firm's unique position."

– Mary Hendrix, Director of Marketing and Business Development, Jackson Kelly

"This work contains valuable 'real life' examples from firms of various sizes on what has worked for them and what has not in project management implementation, training and integration. It will prove to be **an invaluable resource** for any firm that is beginning the process of launching a project management initiative."

– Tea Hoffmann, Chief Strategy Officer, Parker Poe

"Very insightful and useful information. A **must-read** for any lawyer who wants to understand project management and maximize results from alternative fees."

– Erin Corbin Meszaros, Chief Marketing Officer, Burr Forman

"One of the best books on the market—**truly comprehensive**, and not just theoretical like other books on this topic. It will help law firms to make immediate changes."

– Kristin T. Sudholz, Chief Value Officer,
Drinker Biddle & Reath LLP

"A **great reference** for both law firm and in-house personnel… This book provides fundamental insights into the latest practices in legal pricing and project management."

– Keith Maziarek, Senior Project Manager, Strategic Initiatives,
DLA Piper LLP (US)

"The business of law is experiencing epic, once-in-a-lifetime changes. The forces in play have created a 'perfect storm' that should make any sane lawyer uncomfortable. Understanding these forces and learning how to navigate through this storm is essential for survival. Jim's latest book is **an essential resource** for those who desire to understand what is happening and why, and who wish to learn how to take advantage of this upheaval to build a stronger practice."

– Patrick Lamb, Founding Member, Valorem Law Group

"This book **distills complicated issues** into a language that non-economists and non-MBAs will process and understand."

– Scott Wagner, Partner, Bilzin Sumberg

"A very well-written, clear overview and **an important publication**."
– Susanne Mandel, Chief Business Development & Marketing Officer, Lowndes Drosdick Doster Kantor & Reed

"Right on target… offers **a wealth of interesting, compelling, and practical information**. I enjoyed the book and recommend it to my colleagues."
– Ginevra Saylor, National Director, Knowledge Management, Fraser Milner Casgrain LLP

"A terrific resource that **synthesizes the latest and best thinking** about legal project management, pricing, and AFAs, and most importantly, provides practical, actionable recommendations."
– Mark Williamson, Principal, Gray Plant Mooty

"A **great resource** for those getting started and for those in the midst of using LPM and AFAs in their practice… Very straightforward and readable… I appreciated the casual conversational nature of the writing, along with the formality and detail of the citations to other sources. It is a nice mix that makes the text a quick read, but also a resource guide for more detailed research and study of the topics."
– Paul A. Williams, Partner, Shook Hardy & Bacon

"It is no longer sufficient for lawyers to have access to information; they must learn to process and leverage information in disciplined and efficient ways. **This book shows the way.**"
– Daniela Bassan, Partner, Stewart McKelvey

"Jim has done it again. This is **a brilliant piece of work.**"
– Patrick McKenna, Principal, McKenna Associates Inc.

LEGAL PROJECT MANAGEMENT, PRICING, AND ALTERNATIVE FEE ARRANGEMENTS

What firms are doing

By Jim Hassett, Ph.D.

LegalBizDev

www.legalbizdev.com

ISBN 978-0-9886575-0-2

Cover design by Ginny Weaver (www.ginnyweaver.com)

Dedication

This book is dedicated to the members of the LegalBizDev Project Management Advisory Board listed below and to the others who chose to remain anonymous. Their reviews of earlier drafts led to many improvements.

Loretta Auer, Chief Information Officer, Fish & Richardson P.C.

Daniela Bassan, Partner, Stewart McKelvey

Jeff Berardi, Chief Marketing Officer, K&L Gates

Carina Bittel, Director of Administration, Clark Wilson

Steve Blackwell, COO, Thompson Coburn

Keith M. Borack, Global Director of Project Communications, Shearman & Sterling LLP

Toby Brown, Director of Strategic Pricing & Analytics, Akin Gump Strauss Hauer & Feld

Jeff Bukowski, Shareholder, Stevens & Lee

Bruce Clearing Sky Christensen, Executive Director, Warner Norcross & Judd

Thomas S. Clay, Principal, Altman Weil

Jonathan Cooper, Partner, Tucker Ellis

Kim Craig, Director of Legal Project Management Office, Seyfarth Shaw LLP

Stuart Dodds, Director, Global Pricing and Legal Project Management, Baker & McKenzie

Sharon G. Druker, Partner, Robinson Sheppard Shapiro LLP

Caroline Ferguson, Advisor (Digital and Business Improvement), Allen & Overy LLP

Sam Goldblatt, Partner, Nixon Peabody

Jim Hannigan, Project Manager, Fenwick & West

Susan Hastings, Partner, Squire Sanders (US) LLP

Joe Hatley, Partner, Spencer Fane Britt & Brown LLP

Mary Hendrix, Director of Marketing and Business Development, Jackson Kelly

Tea Hoffmann, Chief Strategy Officer, Parker Poe

Gail Huneryager, Director of Business Development, Crowe & Dunlevy

Patrick Johansen, Director of Business Development, Brinks Hofer Gilson & Lione

Byron Kalogerou, Partner, McDermott Will & Emery

Rick A. Kathuria, Director, Project and Vendor Management Office, McCarthy Tétrault LLP

Howard Kaufman, Counsel, Fasken Martineau

Peter Krakaur, Chief Knowledge Officer, Orrick, Herrington & Sutcliffe

Patrick Lamb, Founding Member, Valorem Law Group

Ronald J. Levine, Partner, Herrick, Feinstein LLP

Paul Lippe, CEO, Legal OnRamp

Sara Brooke Littauer, Director of Professional Development and Training, WilmerHale

Monte Malone, Chief of Practice Management, Fulbright & Jaworski

Susanne Mandel, Chief Business Development & Marketing Officer, Lowndes Drosdick Doster Kantor & Reed

Keith Maziarek, Senior Project Manager, Strategic Initiatives, DLA Piper LLP (US)

John McGann, Partner, Wilson Elser

Patrick McKenna, Principal, McKenna Associates Inc.

Erin Corbin Meszaros, Chief Marketing Officer, Burr & Forman

Kelly Milius, AFA Professional Support Lawyer, Perkins Coie LLP

Darrell G. Mottley, Shareholder, Banner & Witcoff, Ltd.

William A. Nolan, Managing Partner, Columbus Office, Barnes & Thornburg

Ron Paquette, Senior Financial Analyst, Holland & Knight

John Paris, Partner, Williams Mullen

Bob Parker, Department Operating Officer, Foley & Lardner LLP

Michael Renetzky, Partner, Locke Lord

Bob Robertson, Director of Strategic Business Development, Cadwalader, Wickersham & Taft LLP

Richard G. Rosenblatt, Partner, Morgan, Lewis & Bockius

Michael Roster, former Managing Partner, Morrison & Foerster's Los Angeles office

Ginevra Saylor, National Director, Knowledge Management, Fraser Milner Casgrain LLP

David S. Schaefer, Managing Partner, New York Office, Loeb & Loeb

Brittaney Schmidt, Senior Manager—Business Development, Vorys, Sater, Seymour and Pease

Kristin T. Sudholz, Chief Value Officer, Drinker Biddle & Reath LLP

Clinton Swan, Head of Marketing and Business Development (Asia Pacific & Middle East Region), Clyde & Co

Craig Townsend, Partner, Adams and Reese

Scott Wagner, Partner, Bilzin Sumberg

Anne Nicholson Weber, Professional Development Manager—Litigation, SNR Denton

Mark White, Chief Administrative Officer, Baker Botts

Paul A. Williams, Partner, Shook Hardy & Bacon

Mark Williamson, Principal, Gray Plant Mooty

Table of Contents

Preface: About this book 1

Chapter 1: Changes in the legal profession 5

Chapter 2: Why is LPM so important? 13
  The benefits of LPM 15
  Defining LPM 21
  LPM and process improvement 23
  LPM and knowledge management 26
  Some historical background 28
  Is LPM just a fad? 31

Chapter 3: Eight key issues in LPM 37
  The eight issues 38
  Perfect is the enemy of good 42

Chapter 4: A variety of approaches to LPM 47
  Seyfarth Shaw 48
  Dechert 52
  Nixon Peabody 54
  McDermott, Will & Emery 56
  Fenwick & West 58
  Baker & McKenzie 58
  Tucker Ellis 59
  Fasken Martineau 60
  Foley & Lardner 61

Chapter 5: Case studies in behavior change 63
  How to maximize the impact of training 67
  Squire Sanders: Certification and client/firm collaboration 72
  Williams Mullen: Just-in-time training plus a course 77
  Gray Plant Mooty: Just-in-time training 81
  Bilzin Sumberg: Just-in-time coaching 87

Chapter 6: Pricing theory 95
  The cost-plus approach 99
  Using cost information to estimate prices 106
  Price competition, discounts, and loss leaders 109
  Value pricing basics 112

Ron Baker's eight steps to implementing value pricing 116
Five ways to improve pricing 119

Chapter 7: How law firms are changing their pricing 123
The rise of the pricing function 124
Using metrics to define value 129
Statistical variation in metrics 134
Where firms are today 135
Predicting the future of pricing 137

Chapter 8: Alternatives to the billable hour 143
AFA surveys 147
AFA profitability 150
Predicting the future of AFAs 155

Chapter 9: Types of AFAs 157
Nine common types of AFAs 157
Are blended rates AFAs? 164
About fixed fees 166
About contingent fees 171
Value adjustment line 174

Chapter 10: Conservative vs. aggressive approaches to AFAs 177
Conservative risk avoidance 177
Aggressive risk-taking 180
Differences of opinion about shadow billing 182

Chapter 11: Using AFAs to develop new business 185
Examples of AFA marketing 185
Proactive AFA marketing 192

Chapter 12: Putting it all together 195
AFAs and pricing 195
AFAs and LPM 198

Chapter 13: What should you do? 203

Appendix: The mathematics of pricing 209
Partner profits and client perceptions 209
Some pricing formulas 216
Discounting revisited 219
Maintaining profitability 221

Endnotes 225

Index 237

About the author 245

Preface

About this book

A draft of this book was reviewed by more than 60 members of the LegalBizDev Project Management Advisory Board. After I read all their comments, it became clear to me that I cannot predict which part of this book will be most valuable to you.

The legal profession is changing, and our reviewers had different needs. Some were most interested in the big picture overview in Chapters 1 to 3. Others preferred the details of what firms are doing about legal project management in Chapters 4 and 5. Still others thought the most useful chapters were in the discussions of pricing (Chapters 6 and 7) or alternative fee arrangements (Chapters 8 to 12).

This has an important implication for every reader: different people will benefit by focusing first on different chapters. So I recommend that you do not read this book from front to back. Instead, go to the table of contents, find a chapter that looks interesting, and start there.

Although this book is being published for the first time, I think of it as a third edition since some of this material appeared previously in the first and second editions of our *Legal Project Management Quick Reference Guide*.

What is new is the way this book integrates the latest thinking and research on the relationships between project management, pricing, and alternative fees.

The second edition of the *Legal Project Management Quick Reference Guide* included two types of material: a comprehensive overview of what law firms were doing to adapt to a changing world, and a "how to" guide with checklists, templates and tools. Lawyers used the tools in our coaching and training programs, as they identified the tactics that will have the most practical and immediate benefits for each individual.

The *Legal Project Management Quick Reference Guide* was first published in 2010, and the field has grown so rapidly since then that we decided the two types of content now need to be divided into two separate books. This book provides a big picture overview of how leading law firms are transforming the way they plan, manage, and price legal work. If you are looking for a "how to" guide that shortens the path from concepts to implementation, you will want to see the book we use in our coaching and training, the third edition of our *Legal Project Management Quick Reference Guide*.

Some sections of this book update and consolidate information which has previously appeared in my blog *Legal Business Development* (at www.jimhassett.com) and in articles that have been published in *Managing Partner* magazine, *Of Counsel*, and other sources. Portions of this book also adapt two articles I wrote with Jonathan Groner for *Bloomberg Law*—"Legal Project Management in the Trenches: What Lawyers Are Doing Today to Increase Efficiency" and "Using Alternative Fee Arrangements to Increase New Business"[1]—and an article I wrote with my brother Matt Hassett for *Legal Management* entitled "Ten years later: A look back and ahead a decade after the ABA Commission on Billable Hours report."[2]

Chapters 6 and 7 on pricing started from the white paper *Legal Pricing in Transition: How Client Demands and Alternative Fees Are Changing the Way that Law Firms Price their Services*, which I also wrote with my brother Matt. For this book, Matt and I expanded and updated some of the ideas in that paper. We talked about whether this meant he should be identified as the co-author of the entire book, but Matt generously declined.

I owe an enormous debt to the rest of the LegalBizDev team, especially to Steve Barrett and Mike Egnatchik. They reviewed every word in several drafts of this book and made many suggestions which I adopted as my own.

This book is certainly not the final word on these topics. No book ever could be, since the field is constantly evolving and new ideas are constantly being tested.

But, as noted in Chapter 3, "Perfect is the enemy of good." This book has many ideas that can help you immediately improve your approach to LPM, pricing and AFAs based on what other lawyers have learned. All you need to do is to act on them.

Jim Hassett
January 2013
Boston, Massachusetts

Chapter 1
Changes in the legal profession

The legal profession is in the midst of historic change. This book will help you decide what to do about it.

But I know you are busy, so I'd like to ask you not to read the chapters in order. As I mentioned in the preface, lawyers find themselves in very different places with regard to this changing marketplace, and different chapters in this book will be most valuable to different lawyers.

For example, if you already accept the need for legal project management (LPM) and are familiar with its definition and benefits, you may want to jump ahead to Chapter 4 to read exactly what law firms are doing about it, or to one of the later chapters on pricing or alternative fee arrangements (AFAs). On the other hand, if you would like to start with a big picture overview, you are in the right place.

Law firms are changing because clients are forcing them to. Very simply, clients are demanding more. In the *2012 Chief Legal Officer Survey,* Altman Weil asked general counsel and others to rate the things "You would most like to see from your outside counsel."[3] The top three answers were greater cost reduction (59%), non-hourly based pricing structures (53%), and more efficient project management (53%).

These three requirements are related to the three part title of this book: legal project management, pricing, and alternative fee arrangements. They are changing the way legal work is performed, and reducing the demand for lawyers. Meanwhile, the supply keeps going up. Clients are spending less, and the result is a worldwide game of legal musical chairs, with a growing number of lawyers being left with nowhere to sit down.

When I began working with lawyers in 2005, the first presentation I went to was about an RFP that Tyco had issued to increase the value their law firms provided.[4] Before then, Tyco had used 167 different law firms for product liability cases. The RFP was designed to combine all that work within a single firm to maximize efficiency. To me, the most interesting fact was that when Tyco made their choice, they selected a firm that was not one of the 167: Shook, Hardy & Bacon, a firm that they had no previous relationship with.

In the years since, the relationship has grown and Shook Hardy now provides a wide array of legal services for product liability and general liability. That is not to say that building a partnership was easy. An ABA Journal article about the relationship quotes partner Paul Williams who "admits the learning curve for Shook Hardy was steep."[5]

This book was written to help reduce that learning curve, at a time when 46% of law departments report that they are working with fewer law firms than they were five years ago, and another 16% report that the number of firms is the same, but that they have switched to different ones.[6] When the music stops, you may need some new skills to make sure you still have a place in the game.

This book could even help you save your firm.

You think your firm is perfectly safe now? That's what the lawyers and staff thought at Dewey & LeBoeuf; Howrey; Heller Ehrman; Thelen Reid & Priest; and Thacher Profitt & Wood. Each of these firms had hundreds of lawyers a few years ago, but now the firms are gone. A large number of smaller firms have died as well.[7]

Every law firm that has gone out of business had its own unique problems. But people often use this as an excuse to say: This could never happen to us. Actually, it could.

When the *American Lawyer* ran a cover story on Dewey's demise they interviewed nearly three dozen former partners and staff and conducted detailed reviews of documents ranging from audited financial reports to the firm's bond offering circular. They concluded that "Dewey's death was the product of years of bad decisions, and of greed on the part of senior partners."[8] The implication for lawyers at other large firms was: Don't worry. It was just a few bad eggs. You are safe.

I have no reason to doubt the facts quoted in the *American Lawyer*, but I interpret them differently. Dewey failed because its leaders were overly optimistic that the kinds of strategies that had worked in the past would continue to work in the future. While I would not argue that this particular bankruptcy was related to AFAs or LPM, I do believe that it was based on a failure to adapt to a changing world.

Dewey's business decisions would not have led to bankruptcy a decade ago. Bad decisions simply did not lead $900 million dollar firms to fail at a time when larger economic forces were pushing all large law firms up.

Ten years ago, there was a lot of room for error. Now there isn't. And as economic pressures have continued to mount, law firms are making more mistakes. For example, in an influential series of blog posts entitled "Growth is Dead," Bruce MacEwen has written about:

> "Suicide pricing" in response to RFPs. These are bids—from name-brand firms, mind you—that are so breathtakingly low one wonders how they could possibly make any money. The short answer is they can't. These bids come in 5, 10, 20, 40% under what my clients think would be reasonable for the matter. But… firms in an industry with excess capacity face an almost irresistible compulsion to cut prices, even to unprofitable levels. The goal is simply to keep people busy, in service of keeping the firm alive and satisfying clients, and in the hope that once market conditions recover, everything can get back to normal.[9]

We have bad news. This IS normal. The new normal.

Large law firms got very comfortable in the first few years of the twenty first century, with constant expansion and ever rising salaries. But, as Microsoft founder Bill Gates put it: "Success is a lousy teacher. It seduces smart people into thinking they can't lose."[10]

In other industries, many people have experienced great success and thought they couldn't lose. Here are some of the companies they used to work for: TWA, Pan Am, Eastern Airlines, MCI WorldCom, American Motors, Montgomery Ward, Woolworth's, RCA, Compaq, Digital Equipment Corporation, Wang, Drexel Burnham, E.F. Hutton, PaineWebber, and Lehman Brothers.

But the world changed, they didn't, and now all those companies are gone. So are many others.[11]

In the last few decades, the forces of global economic change and technology have radically transformed such industries as telecommunications, airlines, retail, mass media, and medicine.

These same forces are now beginning to transform the business of law. According to Richard Susskind, "The legal market is in an unprecedented state of flux. Over the next two decades, the way in which lawyers work will change radically… Unless they adapt, many traditional legal businesses will fail."[12]

There are many lawyers who doubt this message. They believe that there is no need for change, because the good old days will be back soon. But law firm leaders know better.

In the *2012 Law Firms in Transition Survey*, Altman Weil asked 238 managing partners and chairs of firms with over 50 lawyers about the permanence of several trends that are affecting the legal profession.[13] At the top of the list was the "focus on improved practice efficiency," which is at the heart of the LPM movement. 96% of law firm leaders thought that this was a permanent change in the practice of law. When have you ever heard of 96% of lawyers agreeing about anything?

Altman Weil has been doing that survey every year since 2009, comparing how opinions have changed on 10 trends in that time period. All 10 were seen as more permanent in 2012, starting with more price competition (92% saw this as permanent in 2012 vs. 42% in 2009), more commoditized legal work (84% vs. 26%) and more non-hourly billing (80% vs. 28%).[14]

In addition, 60% of law firm leaders thought that the pace of change will increase in the future.

As Seyfarth Shaw chairman Steve Poor explained:

> The pressure on in-house counsel to deliver better services using fewer resources has never been more

> intense. In order to meet business demands, corporate counsel are increasingly looking for firms that deliver greater value. Looking out on a landscape that includes a wider variety of choices than ever before—regional firms, national firms, global firms, virtual firms, legal outsourcing providers and contract firms, among others—their purchasing decisions continue to evolve.
>
> If the recent recession teaches anything for the legal industry, it is this: The changing demands of our clients require the legal services profession to find different paths to deliver value to those who buy our services.[15]

But change is never easy, and this will require both inside and outside counsel to make a substantial investment in learning new skills and experimenting with new ways to do business. As Harry Trueheart, the chairman emeritus of Nixon Peabody, said, "Law firms will pay dearly as we as a profession learn to do this. There will be winners and losers."[16]

It will be easy to lose. Just ignore the need to focus on meeting client expectations and changing lawyers' behavior. The very best way to go too slow is to form a committee to study change. Everybody else can keep acting the same way they always have until the committee agrees on what should be done.

Winning will be a lot harder. Lawyers who have built their careers on delaying action and avoiding risks will now have to learn to act fast and take risks.

Lawyers must accept a new entrepreneurial environment in which they embrace change and stop waiting for others to go first to establish precedents. They must be willing to make mistakes as they innovate to better meet client needs.

As Nobel Prize winner Niels Bohr famously put it, "It is very hard to predict, especially the future."

There are no simple answers; although you will find clear recommendations at the end of Chapters 6 (for pricing) and 13 (for AFAs and LPM), nowhere in this book will you find a list of "twelve easy steps that will save your career."

Instead, this book is a snapshot in time of what lawyers at other firms are doing to adapt to a rapidly evolving marketplace. Understanding what others have learned will help you to figure out the next steps that will work best for your practice, your clients, your firm's culture, and your personality.

Chapter 2

Why is LPM so important?

In one sense, any lawyer who has ever planned a budget or managed an associate has acted as a project manager. But a new movement is now underway to improve legal project management (LPM) by applying formal methods that have been used for decades in engineering, construction, information technology, government contracting and other businesses.

When ALM Legal Intelligence published a 2012 survey of LPM, their first question asked lawyers, “Does your firm employ legal project management processes to its casework?”[17] 51% said yes.[18]

Is the glass half full or half empty? The answer you give may say more about your personality than about the facts.

But from our perspective, it is worth noting how quickly LPM has spread. A few years ago, no one was selling surveys about LPM, and a question like this would probably have been greeted by blank stares, followed by the question: What do you mean by LPM?

In November 2009, Paul Lippe posted this query on Legal OnRamp: "I am at a Law Firm Managing Partners Conference in Toronto and the question just came up on how can law firms learn about Project Management. Any thoughts?"

Just four people responded. Of the four, I was the only one who mentioned a legal project management training program which we were then conducting. If Lippe posted that same question now, so many consultants would rush to describe their training that Legal OnRamp's servers would crash.

On March 19, 2010, I published AmericanLawyer.com's first article on the topic, "Teaching Lawyers How to Manage: Can It Improve the Bottom Line?"[19]

Two weeks later, on April 2, 2010, Law.com shook up the legal project management world with an article titled, "Dechert Puts Its Attorneys through Project Management Training."[20] The article announced the completion of project management workshops for every partner at Dechert.

Lawyers love precedent, and all of a sudden project management proponents had one. The idea that an AmLaw 50 firm was training every one of its lawyers inspired a fear of falling behind. Many firms discovered a sudden interest in the topic, and many consultants discovered a sudden expertise.

In the few short years since, firms have gotten to the point where more than half are using it. Why has it spread so fast?

The benefits of LPM

The reason LPM is growing so rapidly is that it helps law firms meet client needs and their own needs.

When ALM Legal Intelligence surveyed LPM users, they provided a list of 13 benefits and asked, "Which of the following benefits has your firm realized from its project management effort?" Every item on their list was realized by at least 20% of the group. Their most common benefit—"More productive relationships with clients"—was achieved by 62%.

The survey concluded that, "LPM can help bring increased effectiveness, reduce wasted time, and manage client expectations… Those that can successfully implement LPM will find over time that they gain a competitive advantage."[21]

The benefits of LPM include:

- Protect business with current clients
- Increase new business
- Increase the predictability of fees and costs
- Minimize or eliminate surprises
- Improve communication with clients
- Manage risk
- Increase profitability
- Improve realization
- Deliver greater value to clients

Which benefit is the most important? It depends on whom you ask.

Mike Roster, the co-chair of the ACC Value Challenge committee, has a unique perspective on the current changes in the profession. In his work as a practicing lawyer, he managed large legal teams from both sides of the table, as former General Counsel at Stanford University and Stanford Medical Center, and as the managing partner of Morrison & Foerster's Los Angeles office.

Roster often gives a talk entitled "Facing Realities," and his key slide lists three targets that law firms must meet to stay competitive in today's increasingly challenging environment:

1. Reduce clients' total legal costs (either compared to recent experience or to an industry benchmark)

2. Provide high predictability

3. Improve outcomes (for example, reduce the average cost of verdicts and settlements for specific types of cases or reduce the number of workplace disputes that arise in the first place by some target percentage)

"You've got to provide at least one to stay in the game," Roster says. "You will need to provide all three to win." In his view, LPM is most effective when both sides agree on at least one of these goals in advance so that LPM is being used to achieve something specific.

Others emphasize the role of LPM in risk management.

Professional liability insurance is one of the top operating costs for most firms, and its cost keeps going up.

When underwriters set the rates for a particular firm, one factor they take into account is how well the firm manages risk. LPM can reduce professional liability risk many ways, including helping lawyers to control quality, to meet critical deadlines, to avoid or quickly resolve fee disputes with clients, and to maintain active, open and timely communications with clients on all aspects of every engagement.

For example, *Risk Management* magazine quoted Stuart Pattison, a vice president at CNA (one of the largest commercial insurers in the US), about the insurance implications of properly defining legal scope:

> A well-drafted engagement letter can spare future turmoil by spelling out the precise nature of professional services including the attorney handling the matter, specific duties that are not covered, a time-frame and a definition of who the firm will—and will not—be representing… Professional liability insurers now consider a well-established risk management program as a pre-requisite for insuring a legal practice.[22]

According to Bob Feagin, formerly managing partner at Holland & Knight and now special counsel at Paragon Risk Management Services Ltd., "Project management is the key to improving client service, and client service is the key to managing risk. When law firms succeed in managing risk and reducing losses, that has an undeniable impact on lower rates."

While some say that achieving a client/firm joint goal is the most important benefit of LPM, and others stress risk management, a third group focuses on its impact on AFAs and realization.

Lawyers need a reason to be interested in LPM, and the simplest and most common reason we've seen is that a firm has committed to a fixed fee. Nothing gets a lawyer's attention better than knowing that if they go over budget, they will have to pay for it themselves.

As compelling as AFA pressures are, it is important to note that AFAs represent as little as 15% of law firm revenue (see Chapter 8), so the revenue impact of LPM is likely to be far larger for hourly work than for AFAs.

In hourly work, the most direct link between LPM and profitability is in its impact on improved realization.

Anyone who has been involved with law firm finances knows that the *realization rate* is critical to every firm's success. There are three main types: billing realization, collections realization, and total realization.

Billing realization compares what is actually billed to a client to what could have been billed. More formally, billing realization is equal to the amount billed to a client divided by the value of the time recorded on the matter. There are two main ways to calculate the value of the time, one based on the actual rates negotiated with a particular client, the other based on standard hourly rates. Collections realization is more straightforward and compares what clients were billed to what they actually paid. Total realization combines the effects of billing and collections realization in a single figure. (A brief example of the calculations behind these rates can be found in the appendix.)[23]

In many firms an individual lawyer's realization rate will affect her compensation, and the firm's overall rate has a significant impact on the bottom line.[24]

The best available public data on law firm realization is published by Thomson Reuters. Its Peer Monitor Index is based on reported results from 116 large law firms including 45 from the AmLaw 100, 41 from the AmLaw second hundred, and 30 others. Their key measure is called "collected realization rate against standard" and refers to the "percentage of work performed at a firm's standard rates that is actually billed to and collected from clients."[25] According to a recent report,

"Realization has now been falling fairly steadily for more than three years… Realization reached another new all-time low, with net collected realizations falling just below 84%."[26]

This figure represents a serious financial issue and a danger sign. Legal project management (LPM) can help solve the underlying problems.

Many lawyers think of LPM as a way to improve performance on fixed price matters, and it is. But the vast majority of legal work is performed on an hourly basis, so at the end of the day its impact on improved hourly realization could be more significant.

Consider, for example, this common scenario: A client asks her lawyer how much it will cost to handle a particular matter. The lawyer replies that she really can't say because so many different variables are involved. The client says, "Yeah, yeah, I know. But my board keeps asking me for the number. What should I tell them?" After additional hemming and hawing, the lawyer finally says, "Well, in the past, in situations like this we've seen costs ranging from $80K to $110K."

The client hears, "I will do this work for $80K," and passes that number along to the board.

The lawyer begins the work, and for the next few months everything seems fine. Until the matter ends and the client receives a bill for $135K. "I can't pay this bill," she says. "You told me it would cost $80K, and that's what I told my board. If it was going to cost more, why didn't you say something sooner?"

An awkward negotiation drags on for months, and the client ultimately pays $90K. The firm has to write off the other $45K. The billing realization rate on this matter is 66.7% ($90,000 divided by $135,000). No one is particularly happy with the result, and the relationship and the chances of future business have been damaged.

This situation might have been avoided by applying LPM. Our approach is based on eight key issues we first published in 2009 (see Chapter 3), and which have since become widely accepted:

EIGHT KEY ISSUES IN
LEGAL PROJECT MANAGEMENT

1. Set objectives and define scope
2. Identify and schedule activities
3. Assign tasks and manage the team
4. Plan and manage the budget
5. Assess risks
6. Manage quality
7. Manage client communication
8. Negotiate changes of scope

If the relationship partner had taken some time at the start to clearly define scope, both the client and the law firm would have had a better idea of what was and was not included in the cost estimate. If she had planned the budget and managed it closely as things went along, at the very least she and the client would have had some warning about the rising cost. If there had been room to negotiate changes in scope, perhaps the client would have paid more. If there had been a hard cap, perhaps there would have been a chance to limit the work to stay closer to budget.

Constant management of client communication and expectations would have been a big help, not just for the realization rate, but also to maintain the relationship. If the lawyer in this scenario had discussed the issues with the client early in the process, she might have gotten a larger payment, or perhaps she could have met the client's true needs with fewer billable hours, and greatly increased client satisfaction.

No one would argue that LPM will end all disputes over legal costs. But it has already started to end some of them.

So what should we conclude is the most important benefit of LPM to law firms? Is it improved realization? Increased new business? Reduced risk? Something else?

You tell me. The answer depends on what you are trying to achieve.

Some readers may feel that given all these benefits, there is no time to waste in jumping ahead to another chapter. For everyone else, the rest of this chapter digs deeper into exactly LPM is, and where it came from.

Defining LPM

The *ALM Legal Intelligence Survey* started from the following definition: "[Legal project management is] the discipline of planning, organizing, securing, and managing resources to achieve specific goals relating to the control and management of legal cases and matters."[27]

This is similar to the definition lawyer Paul Easton proposed when he started the first blog in this area, in April 2009.[28] In his first substantive post, Easton defined LPM as "the application of widely accepted project management standards, such as those promulgated by the Project Management Institute (PMI), to legal matters."

Both definitions are quite accurate in one sense, but we see them as too restrictive, and too likely to get lawyers thinking in terms of certain types of work processes and the software tools to monitor them.

Our definition of the term is much broader: ***Legal project management adapts proven management techniques to the legal profession to help lawyers achieve their business goals, including increasing client value and protecting profitability.***

Thus, we see LPM as an umbrella term that embraces a very wide range of management techniques. If a proven technique can help lawyers accomplish their goals, we say it is part of LPM.

For example, personal time management is not mentioned in most project management courses and texts, nor is it listed in the index of PMI's bible, *The Project Management Body of Knowledge (Fourth Edition)*. But for some lawyers, personal time management is a vitally important skill which can increase value and profitability. So we think it should be included under LPM, and have included it in the tools and templates we use in coaching.

Like the authors of *Project Management for Lawyers*, we believe that "Project management is a tool box—choose only what you need to most effectively manage [each] project."[29] In our view, even the holy grail of five project management processes—initiate, plan, execute, monitor and control, close—may be ignored by some lawyers. The key to success, we believe, is to find the low-hanging fruit, the management tactics that are most likely to help each individual to increase value and/or profitability.

There are still arguments about the value of LPM, and some can be traced to the fact that the people who are engaged in the debate are using different definitions of the term. We are not interested in the purity of LPM's definition; we just want to help lawyers achieve their goals. That's why we consider both process improvement and knowledge management to be sub-categories of LPM, as described in the next two sections.

LPM and process improvement

Six Sigma and Lean have gotten a lot of headlines in the legal world as a result of Seyfarth Shaw's highly publicized success in using them to streamline work. Both approaches originated in the world of manufacturing, and are examples of process improvement techniques which redesign the way work is performed to increase value and efficiency.

However, there has also been an enormous amount of confusion over exactly what these approaches require, and how they are related to each other, and to LPM.

I became aware of the seriousness of this problem a few years ago when the Director of Professional Development at an AmLaw 100 firm asked me to explain the differences between project management, process improvement, Six Sigma, and Lean. This was an extremely sophisticated client who had been researching this area for months, but she had heard so many different claims from competing consultants that she had trouble keeping them straight.

I explained that Six Sigma is built around techniques Motorola developed to eliminate the causes of manufacturing defects and errors. Lean was developed by Toyota to increase manufacturing efficiency by eliminating the "seven wastes" (excess inventory, excess processing, overproduction, transportation, motion, waiting and defects). They are just two examples of a long list of process improvement methodologies used in other businesses, including business process re-engineering, total quality management (TQM) and ISO 9000. (For details on how Seyfarth applied Six Sigma, and refined their approach into Seyfarth*Lean*, see Chapter 4.)

Given our broad definition of LPM in the preceding section, you may not be surprised to learn that we consider process improvement, Six Sigma, and Lean to be specialized approaches that fall under the more general umbrella term LPM. They are simply tools in the belt, to be used in some cases and ignored in others.

Others argue that process improvement is separate from LPM, and must come first. As one consulting company warns on their web page, "You can manage to perfection, produce exactly what you promised for your client, achieve each milestone on time and demonstrate excellence every step of the way. But what if you're managing an inefficient process?... Legal project management doesn't look at the efficiency of the steps in the project itself. What if you could get from A to B in fewer steps, in less time, with less waste, or by spending less money? Once you're thinking like this, you're thinking about process improvement."[30]

To date, only a few law firms have accepted the purist approach of focusing on process improvement before they implement other simpler and cheaper LPM tactics. Of the 108 law firms that responded to an ALM survey,[31] only four said that they had worked with an approach "modeled after Six Sigma (e.g. Seyfarth's Lean Sigma)."[32] This is not surprising, given that Seyfarth spent several million dollars and more than five years on this approach.

One reason process improvement requires so much effort is that you not only have to figure out how things should be changed in the ideal world, you also have to get lawyers to accept the new process and change their behavior. (For some more efficient approaches to behavior change, see Chapter 5.)

It is human nature to want to do things your own way, and behavior change is a challenge in every profession. According to Carl Binder of The Performance Thinking Network, business process consultants often identify better ways to perform work but then they "can't get the damned people to execute the process."[33] This is especially challenging in law firms, since compliance must sometimes be enforced by a powerful central management team, and many law firms don't have a powerful central management team.

Process improvement clearly has a place in re-engineering the way some legal services are delivered, some of the time. It will be especially useful for the types of legal work that include "cookie cutter" steps. A careful examination of the steps in a repetitive work process can reveal opportunities to streamline and increase efficiency.

For example, when Morgan Lewis used process improvement analysis to improve the delivery of mortgage services, they began by identifying defects in the process that did not add value to the client, including excessive staffing, excessive drafting, and internal meetings.[34] Then they analyzed the causes of these defects, and traced some of the problems back to poor data input, lack of standard high quality forms, lack of associate training, and disorganization related to time pressures. Finally, they developed a number of solutions including standard forms, standard operating procedures and standard communication procedures. These changes enabled Morgan Lewis to reduce the cost of delivering mortgage services "often by more than 25%."

But that does not mean that process improvement is the best approach for every problem, and it does not mean that it must come before other LPM tactics. Arguing that you must fundamentally improve a process before you start to manage it is a little like saying that if you have a car that needs a paint job, you shouldn't bother washing it. It's a great example of the adage "perfect is the enemy of good."

If a law firm has the time, the money, and the will to change the fundamental way they provide services, process improvement will certainly allow them to deliver more value. The question is:

do you think that process improvement is the best way to deliver value in a particular situation?

If you think it may be, and you'd like guidance on specific steps and short-cuts, see "Four approaches to business process improvement" in the book we use in coaching and training, the third edition of the *Legal Project Management Quick Reference Guide*.

LPM and knowledge management

If a lawyer wants to identify the exact approach that will allow her to deliver services more efficiently, it can be extremely helpful to know how colleagues have handled similar situations in the past. But lawyers are busy, and sharing information is not their strong suit. Knowledge is often passed on haphazardly, or not at all. The result is that an enormous amount of legal time and energy goes into re-inventing the wheel.

There are dozens of definitions of exactly what knowledge management (KM) means, but all are built around the idea of systematically sharing insights and experiences.[35] Law firms can deliver greater value to clients by identifying useful intellectual property created during earlier matters, and then leveraging that knowledge inside the firm through increased access and sharing.

Like process improvement, KM is often perceived as completely separate from LPM. For example, before we started working with one of our first clients, he asked why we thought his firm should invest their limited budget in LPM rather than in KM. Our answer: You shouldn't. You need both. By our definition, KM is not an alternative to LPM, it is an important part of it.

KM professionals are now applying a wide array of sophisticated technologies to the law including document management systems, email management systems, business dashboards, and tools to assemble documents, estimate fees, and plan matters. In a 2012 survey conducted by the International Legal Technology Association (ILTA), law firm KM professionals reported that the most widely KM used tools collected models and precedents (52%), and legal research and opinions (48%), along with intranets and portals (37%).[36]

Law firms have been working with KM technologies for several decades, and frankly they have experienced varying degrees of success. Technology can do some amazing things, but only if lawyers use it.

However, even at firms that have little or no widely accepted KM technology, it is very easy for lawyers to make progress in KM simply by devoting time and energy to sharing best practices.

Many lawyers have developed forms, checklists, spreadsheets, and a variety of home-brewed tools and techniques to assist them in working more efficiently. Some take these tools and techniques for granted, others think that no one else would be interested. They may not realize that what's automatic to them may be totally foreign to others.

Sharing even the simplest Rube Goldberg-like tools and techniques may be just what another partner needs to begin becoming more efficient. Starting out in KM does not require investing in elaborate software systems or hiring specialized staff. It simply requires that a group of lawyers make a commitment to collect information about best practices, and then share it. If a best practice works for one lawyer, it may work well for others.

That's why initial LPM efforts often include collecting sample engagement letters, budget spreadsheets, time/billing reports, and checklists. When these informal project management tools are shared, two things happen. First, lawyers become more receptive to learning about project management best practices because they see that this is not a new fad, it is a refinement of tactics partners have been using for years. Second, when lawyers have easy access to these documents, they can often find some low-hanging fruit that can easily be adapted to their own practice.

Some historical background

While winning lawyers over to LPM may be based on some very simple steps, it is important to remember that traditional methods of project management offer a rich and deep body of knowledge that is just beginning to be tapped by lawyers. Professional project managers have developed techniques to improve efficiency in fields ranging from engineering to construction, from software development to government contracting. Dozens of textbooks have been published, and a number of universities offer degrees in the field.

Historians have traced the origins of this discipline back several thousand years to the pyramids, the Great Wall of China, and other massive construction projects. When civil engineers in ancient Rome oversaw the construction of a 53,000-mile network of roads, they needed to develop many sophisticated management techniques. Some of those management techniques are still in use today (and so are some of the roads).

The modern discipline of project management was developed in response to schedule pressures during and after World War II. Admiral Hyman Rickover developed the Program Evaluation and Review Technique (PERT) to manage the Nautilus nuclear submarine program in the early 1950s. A few years later, DuPont began developing the Critical Path Method (CPM) to plan the complex process of opening multiple chemical plants. The Apollo program applied these methods and more to put a man on the moon.

In 1969, five professionals formed an organization called the Project Management Institute (PMI) to facilitate communication in this growing discipline. PMI now has more than 600,000 members in 185 countries, organized into dozens of groups and subgroups.[37]

In 2009, if you had reviewed PMI's list of communities, you would have found groups specializing in how to manage projects in aerospace, construction, energy, entertainment, financial services, healthcare, information technology, pharmaceuticals, retail, transportation, and more. What you would not have found in 2009 was a group that focused on the law. PMI's legal project management group began in September 2010. It has signed up over 3,000 members since then, and is still growing rapidly.

But LPM is still an infant discipline, and just about every aspect of it is subject to debate, including the very definition of the term. As the *Canadian Lawyer* put it, "Project management is so new to the legal profession that everyone is still trying to figure out what it can do and how to make it work."[38]

LPM is a new frontier, and pioneers often disagree about the best tactics. Some have even challenged the very idea of a separate field of LPM. For example, in commenting on a blog post entitled "Is it 'legal' project management or just project management?" Jeff Brandt argued that you don't "make a legal call on your legal telephone" or "check your legal email on your legal mobile device… [and] there is absolutely no such thing as 'legal project management.'"[39]

Since I have already used the term LPM dozens of times, starting with the cover of this book, you will not be surprised to hear that I disagree.

When consultants start working with lawyers, many assume that the differences in the legal profession will be slight. Project managers who have been working inside law firms for years have a different view. Legal project management poses many special challenges, including deadlines and court calendars that are outside a lawyer's control and aggressive opposing counsel whose scorched earth tactics may purposely create roadblocks to efficiency. As skeptical litigators like to say, project management techniques may be very effective when you are building a bridge, but engineers don't have somebody at the other end trying to tear it down.

In my opinion, the most critical difference in legal project management comes from the fundamental fact that project managers must learn how to work effectively with lawyers.

A few years ago, David Maister published a classic article entitled "Are Law Firms Manageable?" in the *American Lawyer*. Maister's article opened with these words: "After spending 25 years saying that all professions are similar and can learn from each other, I'm now ready to make a concession: Law firms are different." He went on to describe four major differences at length: "problems with trust; difficulties with ideology, values, and principles; professional detachment; and unusual approaches to decision making."

Near the end of the article, Maister wrote, "If lawyers deal with each other so poorly, why do they do so well financially? My answer is only partly humorous: The greatest advantage lawyers have is that they compete only with other lawyers. If everyone else does things equally poorly, and clients and recruits find little variation between firms, even the most egregious behavior will not lead to a competitive disadvantage."[40]

When the article was published in 2006, large firms were experiencing their best years in history, and few saw a reason to change. But that was before clients began expecting more from their law firms and before a declining economy and reduced corporate legal budgets made the law firm environment much more competitive.

In Chapters 4 and 5, we will review some of the LPM tactics that different firms are currently experimenting with. Some firms are hiring project management staff, some are building tools, some are buying software, some are investing in Six Sigma and process improvement, some are coaching senior partners, some are training every associate, and some are trying other things. All of them are using the term LPM to refer to these very different approaches.

The key word in the preceding paragraph is "experimenting." Lawyers would prefer to act based on solid precedents, models that have proven their worth over decades. But legal project management is a brand new field, and those who wait decades to apply it do so at their own risk.

Given that LPM is relatively new and people don't agree on exactly what it is, it hardly seems surprising that there is still a hard core of non-believers who question its value, importance, and relevance.

Is LPM just a fad?

Some lawyers believe that the entire efficiency movement was based on the economic downturn that started in 2008, and that LPM will go away soon. Others argue that it is part of a shift in the way legal work is performed to better meet client needs. As Squire Sanders partners Stacy Ballin and Mitch Thompson put it in a *National Law Review* article:

> The world has changed, and clients need more than ever from their law firms. They want their lawyers to partner with them to achieve their business goals and deliver

> value, not to merely send them a monthly bill showing how many hours have been spent.
>
> Like every other kind of business worldwide, law firms are becoming more cost-effective and efficient in providing their services.[41]

Clients are demanding LPM. The Association of Corporate Counsel (ACC), which is "the world's largest community of in-house counsel, with more than 30,000 members in over 75 countries," has been instrumental in promoting legal project management, and even offers a course entitled Project Management for the In-House Law Department.[42]

When the magazine *Lexpert* ran an article about LPM in 2011, they discussed a number of successful Canadian programs that had "the potential to cause a fundamental shift of the tectonic plates of the traditional law firm business model."[43] Specifics included efforts at McCarthy Tétrault, Ogilvy Renault (now part of the Norton Rose Group), Osler, and Stewart McKelvey's participation in our Certified Legal Project Manager® program.

However, perhaps in the interest of journalistic balance, the article also quoted skeptic Keith Mitchell, chair of Farris, Vaughan, Wills & Murphy, who said, "Project management is just another 'flavour of the month' idea being pushed on law firms by consultants," and that "Prudent clients have always done this on large matters. It's just that this week it's suddenly being called project management."[44]

Mitchell is certainly not the only one to see LPM as just another fad that will ultimately go the way of pet rocks and TQM, nor the only one to say, "Lawyers have always done this."

In the *ALM Legal Intelligence Survey*, when participants were asked, "What are some of the hurdles to your firm not instituting legal project management?" the top response was "We don't see a need for project management work" (50%).[45] Lawyers think they are doing it already.

According to Bennett Borden, chair of the electronic discovery and information governance section of Williams Mullen, "on the individual level, 99 percent of the lawyers at any firm would say, 'Yup, I'm good at project management.'"[46]

But, by the standards of other professions, they are wrong.

Yes, successful lawyers have always acted as informal project managers. But there has always been a great deal of room for improvement and lawyers are now taking a more systematic and disciplined approach to these issues. They are studying best practices from other firms and other professions, and they are getting better at providing value and protecting profitability.

Some are sure to remain skeptical. Lawyers are very good at skepticism. We have even heard of one well-known consultant who as recently as 2012 was telling his clients that he "had never seen LPM work at any law firm."

This controversy may not go away soon, because we are in a time of transition where people are still figuring out what works, and they don't yet agree even about what LPM is, or how the phrase should be defined. But while some people debate definitions and interpretations, their competitors are figuring out how to take away their clients.

The potential payoff of adapting knowledge from other businesses is enormous. When litigator Jonathan Cooper of Tucker Ellis completed our Certified Legal Project Manager® program, he wrote:

> Project managers are required to plan and to set objectives, up front, in detail. I think that we as lawyers fall down on this. Often we do not sit down, with our

> clients and with our teams, and discuss how to solve the issue. What is the objective? To win at all costs? To settle the case early? To settle the case between X dollars and Y dollars before the end of the year? We often dive right in and just start working…
>
> Part of the problem is fed by the fluidity of litigation. You are never sure what the case will look like at the end. Facts will come out that were unanticipated. Rulings will be made. Strategic choices will be made. However, I think we make this harder than it should be.
>
> Better planning and orientation would lead to a better understanding of the case and fewer surprises… With better budgets, and better ability to see where we are midstream with the budgets, we could have a much better chance of steering toward the expected or hoped-for result.[47]

To succeed in any business, you just need to be a little better than your competition. If your competitors become sophisticated about LPM before you do, they will offer your clients greater value, and they may steal the clients.

If lawyers accept the broad definition of LPM we described above, they could stop arguing about whether it is useful. If you can improve budgets or quality or communication, wouldn't everyone agree that it is useful? This allows people to proceed to the practical question: how should we implement LPM?

The answer is "it depends." What works best varies from firm to firm, from practice group to practice group, and from lawyer to lawyer depending on clients, goals, the firm's culture and the individual personalities involved.

For experts who reject our definition of LPM as too broad, please feel free to use a different term to refer to efforts to increase value and profitability. But in the current environment, whatever term you use, lawyers need to run their businesses better. Individuals, practice groups, and entire firms need to change behavior to better serve their clients and to protect their livelihood. So whatever you decide to call it, you would be wise to get started soon.

If you accept our broad definition, it is clear that LPM is scalable, and is needed every day in every matter by almost every lawyer. The only exceptions would be lawyers who are already perfect, so there is absolutely nothing more they could do to improve client value or profitability.

Unless you are one of the lawyers who is already perfect, we suggest you follow the LPM advice of Camden Webb quoted at the end of this book in Chapter 13: "Don't hold a series of committee meetings for a year and then do a top-down analysis. Just do something."

Chapter 3
Eight key issues in LPM

Legal project management requires fundamental changes in the ways lawyers do business.

Change is difficult for anyone, and it is especially challenging for lawyers who have developed strong habits over several decades. As Richard Susskind noted in his widely quoted book *The End of Lawyers?* "It is not easy to convince a group of millionaires... that their business model is wrong."[48] But the environment is changing, and lawyers must adapt.

Some aspects of legal project management are easy to implement, but others require a fundamental change in mindset, including:

- More upfront planning
- Increased management
- Closer monitoring of spending
- Selective standardization of work processes
- Accepting some risk to lower cost

This chapter explains the fundamental concepts lawyers must focus on as they make this change.

The eight issues

Once lawyers are convinced to change, what should they do exactly?

Unfortunately, there is no simple generic answer. Each lawyer must identify the individual action items that will produce the greatest benefit given his practice, his clients, his personality, and his firm's culture.

We have found that the best way to find low-hanging fruit is to ask lawyers to start by selecting a particular case or matter, and then decide which of the eight issues on the next page offers the most room for immediate improvement. Then we use forms, tools, templates and checklists to identify one or more action items, and jump in. (For some case study examples of how this worked at four firms, see Chapter 5.)

We began using the list of eight key issues in coaching and training, and published it on our web page in 2009. In March 2010, it appeared in an article I wrote for *AmLaw Daily*.[49] Since then, we have been pleased to see the list become widely accepted.[50]

LPM starts with clearly defining the scope of the work at the outset—what is included in the budget and what is not. In our coaching, some lawyers start by creating a statement of work for a new matter, and then building it into their engagement letter and discussing it with the client.

EIGHT KEY ISSUES IN LEGAL PROJECT MANAGEMENT

1. Set objectives and define scope—You must know exactly what is included in the assignment, and what is not.
2. Identify and schedule activities—After scope is clearly defined, the next step is to break down a complex matter into smaller tasks and to schedule them.
3. Assign tasks and manage the team—To maximize efficiency, the right people must be assigned to the right tasks, and performance must be monitored.
4. Plan and manage the budget—Estimating and controlling costs are a challenge in every profession, and this is the most critical area for many lawyers.
5. Assess risks to the budget and schedule—What can you do at the beginning of a matter to mitigate risks and increase the chances that work will be completed on time, within budget?
6. Manage quality—Most lawyers are very good at delivering high quality legal work. However, this becomes more challenging when schedules change and budgets get reduced.
7. Manage client communication and expectations—This is extremely important to clients, and it is an area where many lawyers have room to improve.
8. Negotiate change orders—No matter how well lawyers manage legal matters, sometimes things change. The issue here is deciding when and how to negotiate these changes with clients.

Perhaps the most important issue of all is #2, identifying and scheduling activities. As Erik Verzuh explained in one of our favorite project management texts, *The Fast Forward MBA in Project Management*, "This is the secret of successful project management: Break the project into small, meaningful, manageable units of work."[51]

In the law, breaking down complex matters into sub-tasks is much harder than it looks. In the mid-1990s, a joint group from The American Bar Association, the Association of Corporate Counsel, and PricewaterhouseCoopers introduced UTBMS (the Uniform Task-Based Management System), a group of codes that are used to plan and manage work.[52]

It is critical to think clearly about the deliverables that a client will receive for a particular matter, and the tasks that are required to complete them. Your team will be far more efficient if everyone knows exactly what they must do and how long it should take. A sophisticated work breakdown structure can also help educate clients about the process that is involved, and help to meet their needs.

In our coaching programs, we often work with lawyers to fill out a Matter Planning Template, which outlines the steps for a particular matter at a level which is granular enough to enable management and tracking, but not so granular as to bury lawyers in detail.[53]

Planning and managing the budget is critical as the project proceeds. If other lawyers on your team enter their time only once a month, and you have to wait for reports from accounting, by the time you realize you are over budget, it may be too late. That's why many firms have been tightening rules about daily recording of hours on every matter, and updating their accounting systems to provide more timely information to team managers.

Some participants in our coaching programs focus on planning month-by-month budgets so they know what to expect. Sometimes this is fairly simple, and sometimes it is not. With some lawyers, we spend a great deal of time finding the most cost-effective approach for their practice for analyzing ranges of estimates in high, medium and low cost situations. And we often talk about exactly when to share budget estimates with clients, and when to keep them private.

The Risk Analysis Template in our coaching materials helps lawyers to think efficiently about which risks can be ignored and which need to be planned for, and how to keep things on track.

Improving client communication is another item that lawyers often focus on in coaching, as is negotiating a change of scope when issues first become apparent, rather than waiting until the end of a matter and just sending a bill.

Note that the eight key issues are not a sequential step-by-step list in which number three always comes before number four, and number five always comes before number six. They are instead a set of interactive issues which may arise at different times in the life cycle of a matter.

All of our coaching and training programs are organized around these eight issues, and our coaching and training materials includes many forms, templates, checklists and tips to help lawyers improve each area.

Perfect is the enemy of good

If we lived in a perfect world with unlimited resources, no one would need the eight key issues or project managers. But here on the planet Earth, resources are always limited and managers are constantly forced to make difficult choices.

For example, when computer programmers develop a new product, no matter how good the product may be, someone can always think of a way to make it even better. But each new feature requires time and money. If software companies intend to stay in business, someone must decide which changes are worth making, and which are not. That's why experts talk about the "iron triangle of project management;" every project is constrained by scope, schedule, and budget. If you change one, the others change too.

It is human nature to always seek a better solution and for each of us to add our own personal stamp. It is the project manager's job to keep human nature in check and ensure that projects are completed on time and within budget.

When Voltaire wrote the phrase "perfect is the enemy of good" in the late eighteenth century, he was not thinking about the needs of legal clients. But the phrase is highly relevant to the challenges lawyers face today as they adapt to what Paul Lippe has called "the new normal."[54]

In the "old normal," lawyers developed a culture of perfectionism in which no stone went unturned. When litigators were trained to prepare for a case, they were taught to consider every twist and turn of any argument that could possibly be raised by the other side, no matter how unlikely. When transactional lawyers were taught how to draft contracts, they were encouraged to draft language that anticipated every possible threat that might arise.

Clients seemed to care little about efficiency, and most lawyers did not care at all. In fact, truth be told, the hourly billing model implied that the more inefficiency a client would pay for, the more hours would be billed and the more revenue would be generated.

But the world has changed and legal budgets are tighter than ever before. The phrase "perfect is the enemy of good" is not an endorsement of mediocrity. It is an endorsement of pragmatism and prudence, of analyzing the cost of each action in advance, and proceeding only if that cost can be justified by its return.

In the new normal, clients want to be the ones who make decisions about how to define quality and what they will pay for. Many have concluded that if a perfect legal solution requires more hours and a bigger bill, they would prefer a lower cost legal approach that is simply "good" and meets their most pressing needs.

A few years ago, after I gave a business development speech at a law firm retreat, one lawyer asked how to handle a client problem. He had recently completed an assignment for a real estate developer, and written what he called "the perfect lease." It was one of the proudest moments of his legal career, and his colleagues agreed that he had crafted language that would protect the client's interests under any conceivable scenario.

There was just one problem: the client hated it. Well, they didn't hate the lease; they hated the bill. They also refused to pay it, because they had been expecting a much lower cost.

So this lawyer asked me: How can I make my client understand that the perfect lease was worth the money? My answer: You probably can't. If that's not what the client wanted, it is not perfect. What you need to do is go back to the client, ask a lot of probing questions, and listen. Don't argue, don't talk, just listen. When you understand what they wanted to buy, then you will be in a position to negotiate a price they will pay, and you can try to salvage the relationship so you will get more of their business in the future.

It all goes back to the best practice mentioned above: hold difficult conversations before money is spent, not after.

As consultant Ron Friedmann summed it up:

> Clients often want to know if there are any major risks: "Let me know if there are any boulders in this playing field." Lawyers often hear that and think they need to find not just the boulders, but also the pebbles. The fear of being wrong—and of malpractice—runs deep. "Perfection thinking" makes it hard to approximate, to apply the 80-20 rule, to guide in the right direction but with some imprecision.[55]

The "80-20 rule" is not taught in law school, but perhaps it should be.[56] In this context, it refers to the idea that 80 percent of a task is accomplished in the first 20 percent of the time. That's one reason deadlines are so often missed. People finish the easy 80 percent of the work quickly, and assume that the rest will go just as fast. But it never does.

In business, time is money, and often the best course is to save time and money by stopping before you have achieved the perfect solution. As the Tao philosopher Lin Yutang put it: "Besides the noble art of getting things done, there is the noble art of leaving things undone. The wisdom of life consists in the elimination of non-essentials."[57]

The underlying issue of how to deal with perfectionism is hardly unique to the legal world. The phrase "perfect is the enemy of good" is often heard in other businesses when project managers discuss how to stay on time and within budget.

When the US was racing Russia to the moon in the 1960s, the Americans had a reputation for technological excellence and innovation and the Russians had a reputation for getting things done. Desk signs were therefore printed up for key members of the Apollo engineering team with the words that were engraved over the entrance to the USSR Technical Institute:

Враг хорошего — это лучше.

The rough translation is—you guessed it—"perfect is the enemy of good."

According to one often-repeated anecdote, when US astronauts needed a pen that would write in space, NASA spent over $1 million developing "The Zero Gravity Pen."[58] It was later marketed to Earthlings by the Fisher Space Pen Company because its pressurized ink cartridges were said to write "in zero gravity, upside down, underwater, over wet and greasy paper, at any angle, and in extreme temperature ranges."

Russian cosmonauts faced the same challenge, but they believed "perfect is the enemy of good," so they used a pencil.

This is a great story, except for one little problem: it is not quite true.[59] NASA did not pay for the development of the pen. The patent owner, Paul Fisher, did. And before the Space Pen became available, both Americans and Russians used pencils. But the story is repeated to this day because it is such a vivid illustration of a fundamental truth.

The pitfalls of perfectionism have become more obvious to lawyers as a result of both client pressures to reduce costs and the growth of alternative fees. In a white paper entitled "Creating the

Law Firm of the Future," Ralph Palumbo of Summit Law Group wrote:

> An experienced lawyer is often able to give an answer that has a 90% probability of being correct. If the lawyer spends only a few minutes giving the answer, the lawyer is paid little for his answer—despite the fact that years of experience and a high level of expertise and judgment is required to give a good answer. Paid by the hour, the lawyer is under-compensated for the service provided. If the same lawyer assigns two associates to research the problem and write memoranda on the issues, the probability that the client will get the right answer may increase from 90% to 95%. The lawyer will make much more money and, in a few cases, the improved probability may be worth the extra fees charged. But in most cases, the customer would have been better off to accept the 90% answer and pay less for the advice.[60]

As Patrick Lamb has noted, "'Perfect is the enemy of good' actually requires more, not less, great lawyering because it requires lawyers to exercise judgment and not run down every rabbit hole."[61]

But some lawyers will find it hard to change their ways. Others have concerns about "missing an issue," however remote it might be. Clients may help them make this transition by refusing to pay some bills. As noted in Chapter 2, Thomson Reuters has found that realization is at an all-time low.[62] Could client dissatisfaction with over-lawyering be one of the reasons?

If some lawyers feel that strongly about continuing the perfectionism of the past, there is not a client in the world who would object to having extra hours devoted to their matters, as long as the lawyers pay for them. But if clients are expected to pay the bill, they get to decide what they need.

Chapter 4

A variety of approaches to LPM

In the last few years, law firms have taken many different approaches to LPM, including training partners and associates, installing new software tools, redesigning work processes, hiring non-lawyer project managers, and much more.

If you believe everything you read on the web, you might think that some law firms have completely mastered LPM. Those of us who work in the trenches have a more realistic view. If I had to rate the legal profession's overall LPM progress over the last few years on a scale of 1 to 10, I'd give it only a 2 or a 3. Some individual lawyers and practice groups have earned a much higher rating, but when it comes to entire law firms there is a huge gap between perception and reality. Perhaps marketing departments have done too good a job of publicizing the successes of lawyers who are using LPM while overlooking others in their firm who are disinterested or actively opposed to it.

Anyone who has ever worked at a law firm has seen how independent lawyers can be and how hard it is to get everyone moving in the same direction. When Patrick McKenna and Gerry

Riskin wrote one of the most influential books about managing law firms, the title they chose was "Herding Cats."[63] So it is not surprising that the *ALM Legal Intelligence Survey* reported that, "for many firms, LPM is restricted to particular practices or even particular lawyers. In some cases, it is difficult to evaluate how extensively the concept has rooted."[64]

This chapter will briefly summarize LPM efforts at nine leading firms, to get a sense of what has been accomplished so far. We begin with the two of the best known pioneers: Seyfarth Shaw, for its work with Six Sigma and Seyfarth*Lean*, and Dechert, for being the first to train every partner on LPM. We will then provide additional examples from seven more firms. This is not meant to be the definitive list of the firms that are "best" at LPM, but rather a sample of the range of activities to date.

Longer case studies of four more firms can be found in Chapter 5, which focuses on a just-in-time behavior change approach.[65]

Seyfarth Shaw

Seyfarth Shaw has more than 800 lawyers in 11 offices and is one of the best-known names in LPM as a result of its work with Six Sigma and Seyfarth*Lean*. Their efforts began in 2006, long before most firms were thinking about increasing efficiency. It has led to an enormous amount of publicity, and to new business, including "36 new or expanded client relationships or engagements in one year."[66]

Clients love it because it reduces cost. For example, Seyfarth*Lean* has:

- "Reduced fees by more than 30 percent (compared to a prior firm) in managing the national portfolio of single employment cases for a Fortune 100 national defense contractor.

- "Reduced costs of lease transactions by approximately 15 percent and cycle time by approximately 30 percent for a nationally recognized retailer that leases millions of square feet of space across the US.
- "For a global manufacturer and marketer, improved trademark prosecution productivity 19 percent better than prior firm's performance; foreign counsel disbursements on global portfolio have been 26 percent below budget"[67]

How have these results been achieved? Through a massive change in the way Seyfarth handles legal matters. It all started with a dinner meeting between Seyfarth Managing Partner Steve Poor and DuPont General Counsel Tom Sager to discuss ways to increase efficiencies. Sager suggested that Seyfarth use a management approach called Six Sigma, but also offered this advice: you should not start down this path unless top management is 100% committed to making it work.

Six Sigma is a set of formal business methodologies designed to improve quality. It was developed at Motorola in 1981 to improve manufacturing quality control, and the name comes from its original goal of assuring that for every million parts that were manufactured, only three would be defective. (If you ever took a statistics course, perhaps you remember that in a normal distribution three per million would be six standard deviations—or six sigma—from the mean.)

In the three decades since, Six Sigma has been used by more than two-thirds of Fortune 500 companies to improve quality and reduce costs. It is built around sophisticated tools and methodologies that force people to get to the heart of a problem and figure out how to re-engineer business processes. But like TQM, political parties, and Buddhism, Six Sigma has evolved and expanded in so many different directions over the years that it is hard to characterize as a single methodology.

According to *Six Sigma for Dummies,* the approach is "Not for the faint of heart. It is intense and rigorous, and it entails a thorough inspection of the way everything is done."[68] Would you guess that implementing an approach like this would be fast or cheap? If you guessed *no* and *no*, you are getting warm.

According to Carla Goldstein, when the process started in 2006, "We were dying. [The consultants] came in with these binders of jargon and statistics and numbers and the lawyers' eyes were rolling around in their heads."[69]

But Seyfarth stuck with it. They collected and analyzed an enormous amount of data about past projects in such categories as M&A transactions, real estate acquisitions, real estate leasing, single plaintiff employment litigation, summary judgments, and commercial litigation. In each category, groups of up to 40 lawyers and staff held meetings over several months to define efficient processes and establish guidelines for how long each step should take.

These days, the program is called Seyfarth*Lean*, and is no longer referred to as Six Sigma. The term is derived from a modified "Lean Six Sigma" approach, which can in turn be traced to the "lean production" movement to increase manufacturing efficiency, most famously in Toyota's efforts to eliminate the "seven wastes."[70]

Nearly all of Seyfarth's lawyers and employees, a total of more than 1500 people, have participated in Seyfarth*Lean* training in some form.

Much of Seyfarth*Lean* is built around process mapping, defining the exact steps that are required to perform a process more efficiently. This includes looking at every process from the client's point of view, analyzing whether each step adds value for the client, and eliminating the steps that don't.

This type of analysis has helped Seyfarth discover some interesting and counter-intuitive trends. For example, many general counsel believe that longer negotiations tend to produce better settlements, because it pays to be tough. In fact, when Seyfarth systematically analyzed data from past cases, just the opposite was true: the less time a case was open, the less clients typically paid in the settlement plus legal fees.

To date, Seyfarth Shaw has developed over 300 process maps.[71]

In a Law Technology article entitled "How six big law firms get serious about legal project management," Alan Cohen noted that that, "It can take weeks to create a map, but the result is a template that spells out the various phases of a matter—and an efficient way to do them.[72]

It takes a room full of lawyers and staff several weeks to create one process map, and Seyfarth has developed over 300 so far. So how much did that cost? A few years ago, the American Lawyer reported that, "Seyfarth has spent over $3 million to date administering and training workers... and budgets $200,000-$500,000 annually for such costs."[73]

The cost of this approach, and the time it takes, are two of the reasons it has not been widely adopted by other firms. A third reason was explained by Goldstein and Lisa Damon:

> For [a] successful process improvement you need support from the top. Not only will this encourage people to engage in the analysis to determine the improvements, but it is critical to successfully implement the identified solutions and for the team members to sustain the changes.[74]

Support from the top is extremely helpful for any LPM approach, but for this type of ambitious effort, lack of strong support from a strong leader would be a deal breaker.

Dechert

Dechert has more than 800 lawyers in the US, Europe, Asia and the Middle East. In 2009, to address client demands for more value and timeliness, they began an ambitious training program. As noted in Chapter 2, their April 2010 announcement that they had completed training all partners set off a flurry of activity at other firms that wanted to keep up.[75]

Since then, they have extended the training to all of Dechert's legal professionals, including associates, support staff, and paralegals. Training programs have emphasized client communication before, during, and after the project, and keeping track of project progress with an eye towards milestones and budgets. Many participants have also learned how to map a matter from the start of the project to the conclusion.

Dechert now has a dedicated Director of Project Management, Colleen Nihill, who heads a group with backgrounds in finance, business, Six Sigma accreditations, law, math, and statistics. Using project management tools, they help Dechert partners, associates, and staff to plan, budget, and manage client matters economically and proficiently. The group pores over data, writes reports, and meets with project teams to review project progress and future milestones. "Even though attorneys have access to information on their dashboards, one of the things analysts can do is drill down and write reports specific to [a partner's or client's] needs," says Nihill.[76]

In *Project Management for Lawyers*, Nihill and Dechert partner Ben Barnett have provided an excellent list of six lessons they learned in several years of implementing LPM:

- *"Lesson one—You can't do what you don't define."* At the outset, it pays to get input from all of a project's decision makers and create a plan including the project's objective, tasks and milestones, and the budget.

- *"Lesson two—Building a team to be its best."* Keeping in mind schedule and budget, you must pick the smallest team possible based on their knowledge of the client or matter, their work habits, and past project successes. Don't skip this step and just use the same people you always use. "You should also be ruthless in terms of what resources you really need on your team."[77] As the project continues, keep an eye on team unity and reward good work. If some aspect of the team is not working, fix the problem immediately.
- *"Lesson three—The nuts and bolts."* You must follow the concrete project plan, keeping both the team and yourself on track. Make sure you set a good work example for your team.
- *"Lesson four—Where are we?"* Monitor the progress of the project and keep the client informed about where you are in terms of budget and milestones. Dechert uses several software systems—Thomson Reuters Elite, Redwood Analytics, and Tikit's Carpe Diem—to track budgets and time spent on matters, and to plan new projects with similar budgets or goals. Progress must be communicated to the client to make sure they are satisfied.
- *"Lesson five—Planning for problems."* The project manager must identify problems quickly and find solutions. Managing challenges goes hand in hand with keeping track of the project. "What we have seen is the need not for a monthly retrospective look back, but real-time data so attorneys can make decisions and amendments," says Nihill. "You don't want to be 70 percent through the budget with nowhere near 30 percent of the work left to go."[78]

- *"Lesson six—Delivering success."* "The most critical phase of long-term successful project management happens after delivery of the final product—a step that most often gets short shrift."[79] At the end of the project, hold meetings with both your client and your team, and write up the lessons learned.[80]

Nixon Peabody

Nixon Peabody has approximately 700 attorneys throughout the US, Europe, and Asia.

In the Nixon Peabody Project Management initiative, which began in 2010, Nixon Peabody has trained hundreds of its attorneys and more than 80 of its paralegals and legal technology specialists. They have also created tools to assist with project scoping, budget planning, project/budget tracking, and client collaboration. According to Samuel Goldblatt, former head of litigation at Nixon Peabody and now firm-wide co-chair of its LPM task force, this program has increased client satisfaction and led to a number of new engagements.

As Chief Sales Officer Philip Austin has noted, "[Clients] ask firms to address what they are doing to drive efficiency and increase [cost] predictability; they want to know what specific things you've put in place [to accomplish those goals]."[81]

A common project management platform of established methods and tools such as books, templates, and checklists helps the project management-trained attorneys collaborate with each other and with clients to manage matters effectively. Each matter is tackled in four stages:

1. Outline through discussions and on paper:
    - Objectives

- Scope
- Deliverables
- Client's view of project desired outcome

2. Map out milestones, project phases, time, team resources and roles, communication plan, and budget.
3. Start the work and manage the project. Monitor milestones, budgets, and unexpected problems. Keep lines of communication open.
4. Review after the project ends. Meet with client and team to discuss:
    - What went well?
    - What can we do better?
    - Future projects

Asking the right questions is invaluable. "A questionnaire that asks good questions about how you did may not seem a sophisticated tool, but it's an important one," says Austin. "It lets you plan for future engagements."[82]

For example, an exhaustive discussion between the lawyers and the key executives at the client company is held after each deal or litigation is concluded. The topics, Goldblatt says, include, "How accurate was the budget? If there were changes, could we have anticipated them better? Did the economics work for the client? Did we have the right level of communication with the client during the matter?"

The constructive criticism at these debriefings, Goldblatt says, has often led to discussions of new engagements for the firm: "What is our next project going to be like?"

McDermott, Will & Emery

McDermott Will & Emery has more than 1,100 lawyers around the world. Partner Byron Kalogerou says that when he first started talking about LPM, he felt like he was living out his college motto: "A voice crying in the wilderness." (Kalogerou went to Dartmouth, so naturally the motto was in Latin: "Vox clamantis in deserto.") Fortunately, the world has come around to his way of thinking.

In his work as an M&A lawyer, Kalogerou developed and uses the M&A Gateway, a one stop web-based collaborative deal portal that, according to a McDermott Will & Emery brochure, "Streamlines the M&A process, reducing inefficiencies and costs. The M&A Gateway enables counsel to corral all of the moving pieces of a deal, so that everyone involved knows what needs to be done, by when, by whom and at what cost."

The Gateway was the first-of-its kind application to use a legal project management tool for M&A transactions.

When work begins on a new deal, the client team sits down with McDermott lawyers to perform the kind of basic planning that professional project managers do on any new job: identify tasks, assign people to each task, set deadlines, and plan the budget. The brochure shows how this works for a typical deal, with tasks grouped into four phases: due diligence, negotiations, closing conditions and post-closing.

As the deal proceeds, tasks and issues are tracked online in the M&A Gateway, so that every team member on both sides of the table can find out exactly where things stand, minute by minute, by reviewing the latest updates at a password-protected website. In the brochure's fictional example, several high priority issues are highlighted for action, including "Plant Lease—Right of First

Refusal Grant" and "Determine whether pre-merger filing is required with the Federal Competition Commission in Mexico."

Just as important, a budget for each phase is established online at the beginning of the deal, whether the work is performed on an hourly basis or for an alternative fee. The system then tracks costs to date and compares them to the budgeted estimate. In the fictional example in the brochure, the negotiations stage was initially budgeted at $125K. By the time 75% of the work had been completed, only $85K had been spent. The system calculates the "expected variance" from these figures to show that negotiations could be completed more than $11K under the original budget. (When you do the math, if 75% of the work cost $85,000, 100% of the work would cost $113,333. Subtract that from the original estimate of $125,000 and you will see a net savings of $11,667.)

Kalogerou's development of the Gateway grew out of his 17 years in-house, including 14 years at Tyco, when the company did some $37.5 billion in deals. "We recognized that speed and certainty of closing were key advantages to the way we did deals," Kalogerou said. "I developed the Gateway to streamline the deal process and bring greater deal velocity and predictability to my clients."

Not too many years ago, the idea of using an online system like this to facilitate team communication and to track spending would have seemed far too radical for most lawyers. These days, more and more software tools are springing up to meet clients' demands for increased efficiency.

Fenwick & West

Fenwick & West is a 300-lawyer firm that was founded in Silicon Valley "before Silicon Valley existed." Jim Hannigan is one of the new breed of professional project managers who are not lawyers but are playing an increasing role in planning legal work. He describes the goals of his firm's LPM program very simply as, "Increased client satisfaction, increased realization, and increased productivity leading to more engagements."

One project Hannigan has been involved in is the firm's "historical task coding," in which financial analysts at the firm look back at past matters and use American Bar Association task codes to see how much particular aspects of each case cost and how much time they took. The firm then uses this past data as a basis for future bids in response to RFPs issued by prospective clients.

Another approach that Fenwick & West uses is to require the responsible attorney for every case over a certain amount to produce a budget in advance. To assist the lawyers, the firm employs a staff of four in-house budget analysts.

Baker & McKenzie

Non-lawyers also play a key role in the approach to LPM at Baker & McKenzie, which has more than 4,000 lawyers in over 70 offices worldwide. In 2010, the firm brought in professional project manager Sarah Prime to its London office to help increase efficiency in key matters. Prime often works as a billable member of the client team. In one instance a client requested that she be included on the team because the client "Valued the involvement of a project management resource and saw that it represented a cost effective approach, freeing up lawyer time to deliver high value services."

Prime works not just on individual matters, but also "On wider process efficiency. Both are equally important, as refinements captured on one matter can be fed into subsequent matters."

The key to true efficiency is lawyer behavior and the way things get done. Stuart Dodds, Baker & McKenzie's director of global pricing, explained that is why "Project management training is a key component of our associate and partner skills development, with a number of courses already implemented worldwide."

According to Kirsty Wilson, Baker & McKenzie's global head of reorganization, the result of this broad and deep commitment to LPM is that "Our clients go home happy in the knowledge that throughout each stage of the project there is complete transparency."

Tucker Ellis

Tucker Ellis has more than 160 lawyers in offices in Cleveland, Columbus, Denver, Los Angeles, and San Francisco. Trial lawyer Jonathan Cooper has focused on process improvement, especially budgeting and risk assessment tools to plan litigation costs.

"We've developed software tools that help us estimate well in advance what something will cost, at least roughly, at the RFP stage," Cooper says. "The idea is to turn budgeting more into something like TurboTax."

The software, Cooper says, helps the firm ask questions like, "What are the really expensive points here? Do we really need to depose this expert?"

If you understand the risk, you can assess whether it's worth the potential reward. One result has been that Tucker Ellis, which works mostly in the areas of defending mass tort claims, product liability, and pharmaceutical liability, is now deriving 60% of its revenues from non-hourly alternative fee arrangements.

Fasken Martineau

Fasken Martineau, one of the largest law firms in Canada, is making legal project management a part of the firm's culture through a series of "Lunch & Learn" and "Breakfast Club" sessions in which lawyers experienced in project management train six to eight other firm lawyers at one time.

"The intent is to break down barriers to understanding what LPM is," says Sean Morley, a partner in the business law section.

> In many instances lawyers are intuitively practicing LPM but not always in a disciplined way. We are developing standardized templates to assist in planning, budgeting and budget review, including task lists. We want to make the connection between planning discipline and cost-effective management of legal mandates. The firm is then in a better position to manage the file and to price it with a greater degree of confidence, whether the price is based on hourly rates or on an alternative fee arrangement.

The firm also has introduced a robust legal project management software capability. This will assist its lawyers both in better file management and in facilitating budgeting processes that can engage the client early and often.

Foley & Lardner

Foley & Lardner has over 900 lawyers at more than 20 offices in the US and overseas. David Simon, the former vice chair of strategy and business development for their litigation department, emphasizes a business-oriented approach to the firm's cases.

Historically, he says, litigators have been trained to read every single document that arrives at the doorstep during discovery—but "sometimes a client doesn't want to pay for all that. We work with the client and say, 'Here are the risks, the costs and the benefits. We need to make a judgment that is business-driven.'"

Foley has developed a variety of internal tools to promote this business-driven orientation, including Foley LitAdvantage, a suite of tools that features, among other things, "a Master Checklist for new cases, designed to help firm lawyers tailor litigation work plans to the client's business objectives, and the firm's highly regarded Budget Management Tool software."

Simon says Foley & Lardner's approach is not only good for the client; it can also help differentiate the firm and increase its market share.

"A few years ago, I read the marketing description that we sent to clients," Simon recalls, "and I said, 'Who cares?' Every law firm in the country can say this stuff. We started with what our clients want to hear and built our service delivery model around that. I want to describe our firm in a way that differentiates, and LPM is an indispensable part of that."

The current competitive environment is making this new way of thinking take hold. According to Simon, "When lawyers find that they have lost a client to a firm that is efficient and effective in LPM, they listen."

As Simon summed it up, "It surprises me that more firms aren't doing this already. Litigators need to think about a case from the point of view of the client's business objectives. Corporate clients want more for less.... Your clients are telling you what they want you to do, so just do it."

Chapter 5

Case studies in behavior change

Chapter 4 summarized how firms like Seyfarth, Dechert, Nixon Peabody and others have been applying LPM to deliver greater value to their clients while protecting profitability. All of these firms, and many others not mentioned in this book, have reported significant progress and benefits.

The truth is, in the current legal marketplace, it is easy to obtain benefits from LPM. Historically, lawyers have been trained and compensated to focus only on getting the best legal result. Under the hourly business model, few clients asked lawyers to be efficient, and few lawyers tried.

As a result, as Lisa Damon of Seyfarth Shaw has noted, "If you get a group of lawyers and staff into a room to discuss how to make things more efficient, it's very easy to find savings."[83]

Compared to the habits that developed under the billable hour, almost any systematic procedure will make things better. When evaluating the relative merits of different approaches to training, the key question is: how quickly will lawyers change their behavior, and what will it cost?

These days, law firms are increasingly looking for the tactics that produce the best return on investment, by delivering the greatest impact in the shortest amount of time. We have found that the key to success is to start by focusing on behavior change with a few key attorneys.

When ALM Legal Intelligence surveyed 236 law firm respondents about the best ways to implement LPM, they came to the same conclusion: "Partners most willing to adopt LPM should lead efforts in an incremental manner. The quicker there are demonstrable positive benefits, the faster other partners will take notice."[84]

As Christopher Spizzirri, e-discovery counsel at Morris James, put it in that same survey, "You've got to introduce one element of change at a time and work that. I learned early on that if you try to change too many things at once, you get a lot of resistance."[85]

Professionals in the training business often talk about the importance of distinguishing between two types of goals: education and behavior change. Almost every training program aims at both. But education often fails to change behavior. If you study ten books about how to lose weight, you may become very knowledgeable about what you should and should not do. But you won't lose a pound until you change your behavior.

Organizations get the greatest return on their training investment when they think carefully about the tradeoffs between the two and about which is more important in a particular situation.

Educating is relatively easy, but changing behavior is very hard. It is also the central problem in legal project management. The Association of Corporate Counsel and the ABA recently conducted a meeting "At which leaders of corporate and law firm litigation departments rolled up their sleeves and tackled the complex issues surrounding present day concepts of value in litigation." In an *ACC Docket* article summarizing the event, the authors noted that progress will not be based on improved understanding or increased knowledge. Instead, "The challenge is change/behavior management."[86] It's not a question of knowing what to do, it's a question of getting lawyers to do it.

Many law firms are still focused on traditional programs that educate and transmit information. Attorneys are being trained in LPM, CLE credits are being granted, online courses are being completed, and books and articles are being scrutinized.

The good news about traditional training is that you can finish it quickly. Hold a few large workshops, put out a press release announcing that your firm has made a commitment to LPM, and you're done. It's easiest of all if you focus on training associates and hope that the management lessons they learn will trickle uphill. Most associates will show up, and their grumbling will be more muted than with partners.

The bad news is that if you want to change behavior, traditional training is not enough.

We recommend an approach which is widely used in other professions, but new to law: "just-in-time" training and coaching. Background on this approach appears in the section below on "How to maximize the impact of training." If you prefer to skip the theory and go directly to examples of how it has worked, jump ahead to one or all of the case studies in this chapter, from four clients that have used slightly different tactics to begin changing lawyers' behavior.

At all four firms, we started by helping a few influential partners directly experience the immediate benefits of LPM. Each lawyer focused on the issues that would have the greatest impact for their practice in the short term. They identified clients and concrete action items and began working on them immediately.

Once they saw the results, they became internal champions for LPM and spread the word.

The way they did this, and what happened next, varied from one firm to another. The four case studies are presented in chronological order, starting with the firm we have worked with longest:

- Squire Sanders started by putting one of its most senior litigators through our Certified Legal Project Manager® program, and then proceeded to conduct client/firm collaboration workshops with important clients
- Williams Mullen started with two just-in-time training programs for influential partners, and then had us conduct a course for 30 of their most influential rainmakers
- Gray Plant Mooty focused on the just-in-time training approach, and has run three programs as of the date this account was written
- Bilzin Sumberg took the most ambitious approach and has seen the biggest results. They have offered three months of intensive just-in-time coaching to almost half of their partners to date, including the vast majority of those who manage large matters.

If you don't have time to read this entire chapter, start with the most recent example, the Bilzin Sumberg case study.

At all four of these firms, and at every other law firm on the planet, LPM is a work in progress. As Harry Trueheart, chairman emeritus at Nixon Peabody, put it, "A lot of education will go into this, and it's not cheap."[87]

While true change will be neither fast nor easy, the slow pace of the entire profession can lead to good news when firms begin to make progress. One of our clients contacted us recently to report that she had just won some business as a result of LPM skills developed in one of our just-in-time workshops two years before. She said she was frustrated with the slow pace of change in her firm, but that their competitors were even slower. “If you move like a turtle but you’re racing a bunch of snails,” she said, “It all works out in the end.”

How to maximize the impact of training

When I started LegalBizDev in 1985, the company was named Brattle Systems and we developed custom training programs for government agencies and for companies from American Express to Zurich Financial Services. Over the two decades that we specialized in custom training, the business changed significantly as clients cut back on traditional training budgets and shifted instead towards a more cost effective “just-in-time” approach.

For example, in the late 1980s there was a huge market for people taking classes to learn how to use new software. But these days when people want to know how to use advanced features of Word or Excel, few would consider signing up for a class or even looking up the answer in a book. Instead, they use the convenient “just-in-time” help systems and training tools that Microsoft has built into each program, and simply look up what they need when they need it.

“Just-in-time” training tactics have been applied to almost every field you can think of, including project management. For one example, see the study of “The use of ‘just-in-time’ training in a project environment,” that appeared in the *International Journal of Project Management*.[88] The authors start by pointing out that “Around 40% of the knowledge acquired in training is lost after a break of one month, rising to 90% after six months,” and go on to show how the problem can be solved: by providing access to tools that allow people to solve the problems they care about, just in time.

Given what we knew about what worked best in other businesses, when we saw lawyers recognize the need for LPM training, we decided to apply the "just-in-time" approach. We publicized our approach in March 2010, in the first article AmLaw Daily published on project management.[89]

Two weeks after the AmLaw Daily piece appeared, another article appeared on Law.com announcing that every partner at Dechert had completed project management training.[90] The phones of every LPM consultant started ringing the morning the Dechert article appeared. Over the next several months, we talked to many firms that wanted to take the same approach. We did our best to discourage them.

I particularly remember one RFP which asked us to bid on traditional education course for over 500 lawyers at an AmLaw 100 firm. This was a serious test of how strongly we felt, and we had a spirited internal discussion about whether we should bid.

We asked the client if they would consider focusing their efforts on a smaller number of lawyers, the ones who were motivated to change. The client said no, they wanted to train everyone. We explained that while we thought the top-down "train everyone" approach could have some success, it would be a very expensive way to get modest results and it could even backfire by increasing resistance among some lawyers. In the end, we declined to bid.

These days, almost no one recommends the "train everybody" approach.

However, we do still see law firms that want to identify a complete solution before they will take the first step. Sometimes this takes the form of looking for a project management software system that everyone can use, or a project management professional who will magically fix everything. A committee is assigned, the meetings drag on, and a very long time is spent on thinking rather than on doing anything.

As Toby Brown, the director of strategic pricing and analytics at Akin Gump, has put it:

> It's classic for a firm to "build then do" with software and other systems. A committee attempts to anticipate every need a proposed system might meet before it is developed and rolled out. The thinking has been that more input is better, and the process will insure that new systems meet the needs of all the lawyers in the firm. In my opinion, this has never worked. Design by committee is a recipe for failure. Instead of a focused, functional system, you end up with a bloated one that doesn't address the original need.... Until you start doing legal project management, you are not going to know your software and system needs. Buying and implementing software and establishing policies and processes before you know what you need doesn't make sense. Cart—get thee behind the horse![91]

Instead of looking for the ultimate solution before they take any action, law firms should learn from software developers who use "Agile methods" to develop programs as quickly as possible. They develop a pilot version, try it out on typical users, make changes based on feedback, and try it out again. Rather than spending time on the perfect requirements document, they simply develop release after release until they have a product that truly meets user needs.

Agile concepts have taken hold in many businesses, as an increasingly competitive world has required vendors in every field to move faster and do more with less.

When we were in the custom training business, our clients sometimes required us to follow a formal training development process which demanded that multiple drafts of training materials be reviewed repeatedly by a group of subject matter experts, before they were tried out with a live audience of typical students.

That process did produce effective training programs, but they took a very long time to develop. And they were not very cost effective. In some cases, we developed training modules that were absolutely perfect from the subject matter expert's point of view, only to find that students did not benefit from them. Those modules were dropped from the course and all that development time and money was wasted.

After a few years, we began using a leaner process to get in front of students more quickly by rapidly developing pilot test materials and getting user feedback. This approach was faster, cheaper, and ultimately more effective. That's one of the elements of the just-in-time training and coaching approach that we recommend for legal project management.

In the just-in-time training and coaching programs described in the case studies below, each individual lawyer is guided simply to select action items that fit his or her practice and personality, and give it a try. When they work, do more. If they don't work, try something else.

You won't get a second chance to make a first impression, so you'd better make sure your first legal project management program is well designed and executed. If it fails, you are going to have a tough time building support for the second one.

In a quarter-century in the training business, we have found that the single most important factor in success is selecting the right people to be trained. This is particularly critical in an area like legal project management, where there may be resistance and skepticism about the behavior changes, not to mention more than a generation's worth of inertia.

We recommend starting with lawyers who are open to new ideas and who have the most to gain. That could be the key partners who are responsible for new alternative fee arrangements. It could be relationship partners who are worried about protecting business with key clients that are looking for greater efficiency and increased value from their outside counsel. It could be an entire practice group that is considering new checklists, templates, and processes to improve its competitive position.

The training may not be 100% perfect, but it will pay for itself several times over by enhancing client relationships and profitability. And its success will create a new group of evangelists within the firm who will spread the word that legal project management can help serve clients better.

The exact individuals and groups will vary from firm to firm. But in every case, the best lawyers to start with are those who are open-minded about change and efficiency, in a position to benefit when LPM makes a difference, and influential enough to quickly spread the word of their success.

Examples of the success of this approach appear in the four case studies below.

Squire Sanders: Certification and client/firm collaboration

Squire Sanders is a global firm with approximately 1,300 lawyers in 37 offices and 18 countries. Our work with them began, as it often does, with a presentation at their annual partners meeting. This one was in October 2010, and the topic was legal project management. Afterwards, I got into a discussion with litigator Stacy Ballin, then co-chair of Squire Sanders' Project Management Committee, about the potential value of a high level certification program for senior partners who wanted to lead LPM efforts within their firms.

At that time, Squire Sanders had already been working on LPM for several years and had hired Vince Cordo as their director of value and project management. Ballin told me that her firm's commitment to LPM grew out of the Association of Corporate Counsel's Value Challenge: "We accepted the Value Challenge a few years ago and rolled up our sleeves. The litigation group began by requiring an internal budget for all new cases, even if the client never requested one. We also required a case management plan that all team members could review to increase their efficiency."

Then Squire Sanders opened the process to the client. A custom-designed extranet database called MyMatter contains all the relevant documents for each case—case plans, court pleadings, witness lists, expert information, deposition summaries, engagement letters, budgets, invoices, and more. This gives immediate access to the key documents, in a single location, to the Squire Sanders team, to in-house counsel, and to client representatives.

To illustrate how it works, consider the example of a major international financial services company that is prosecuting a large number of foreclosure cases. Their in-house counsel and executives can access their MyMatter database in real-time and obtain a bird's eye view of the status of every foreclosure case, including valuation determinations, expenses and potential risks. The client can also track the budget for each case and compare it to the legal spend to date.

As a result of my discussions with Ballin and others at the retreat, we designed the first formal program to certify lawyers as legal project managers. When we announced the program in December 2010, Ballin was one of the first to sign up.[92]

The certification program starts with a series of assignments based on required readings from leading project management texts. It ends with a final project to identify the concepts which could have the biggest impact on the lawyer's practice.

As the litigation group business partner, Ballin is responsible for approving discretionary write-downs, where a relationship partner decides not to bill a client for some of the time charged to a case and writes down a portion of the bill before it is sent to the client.

For the final project of her certification program, Ballin decided to review all 2010 litigation write-downs over $10K. She found that a few young partners had unusually high write-down rates, which they explained as simply costs beyond budget or caused by a pattern of inefficiency.

Inefficiency reduces the value clients receive, and discretionary write-downs have an immediate negative impact on the bottom line. So Ballin decided to interview six of these young partners and explore with them how the firm could help them reduce inefficiency and write-downs in the future.

Her project began by developing a phone interview survey questionnaire based in part on the questions she answered in the first part of our certification program. She then "developed a plan as to how to use the results to reduce write-downs in the future, and to measure the financial impact of [her] recommendations." Finally, she used the findings to coach these lawyers and others with similar write-down patterns and found that coaching did indeed improve their realization rates.

Squire Sanders has not revealed its billing realization rate, but with annual revenues over $500 million, an improvement of 1% would mean an immediate increase in profits of $5 million.

One year after the program ended, Ballin was still applying these findings. As she summed it up in an email, "I am finding that building awareness of the need for better project management is best achieved through coaching individual by individual. While that may seem less efficient with respect to time, it works much better than global education."

Around the time that Ballin was being awarded her certificate as a Certified Legal Project Manager®, Squire Sanders became the first firm to sign up for another new program: a client/firm collaboration workshop in LPM.

The program was designed to facilitate collaboration between large law firms and their most important clients by addressing the most fundamental question in the ACC Value Challenge: "Working together, how do we improve the value of legal services?"

As Paul Lippe of Legal OnRamp has noted, "The practice of law has shifted from an individual effort to one emphasizing teamwork and collaboration… When firms had a monopoly on expertise, delivery of service was a one-way street. But now most work involves collaboration and coordination between firms and clients."[93]

The key event in our program was a half-day workshop at the client's office with seven active participants: the client's general counsel and three of his key staff, and three leaders of the Squire Sanders client team that serves them: Dave Grauer, Keith Shumate and Heather Stutz. In addition, three other lawyers sat in as observers.

To start the day, we offered a brief overview of the eight key issues described in the course manual. Then we began a structured brainstorming process to efficiently identify action items: How could LPM principles quickly be applied to strengthen this particular relationship?

The brainstorming produced a list of 19 action items. The biggest category involved improved communication, including scheduling a "lessons learned" review session for one current matter, scheduling regular meetings for both the Squire Sanders team and for the in-house department, and scheduling a monthly call in which Squire Sanders briefed the client on legal trends in their industry, including ideas for enhancing revenue.

Other communication action items involved technology. Some were very simple uses of existing systems, including setting up a new folder on the client's network to simplify internal access to key documents. A few involved new software solutions. As a result of the workshop discussion, Squire Sanders has now begun implementing its custom-designed extranet database, MyMatter, for this in-house department, in order to provide them with immediate access to key documents in a single location.

Five of the 19 action items involved AFAs. Both Squire Sanders and this client were interested in exploring non-hourly AFAs, and the brainstorming process identified several specific steps toward this goal, including making a list of new work where AFAs made sense to both sides.

Does that sound like marketing? It should. The client/firm collaboration workshop is designed to strengthen relationships and increase value, which is a pretty good definition of marketing.

During the workshop, specific individuals volunteered to be responsible for each of the 19 items. Then, for the next 30 days, our coach followed up with participants to provide advice on implementation, along with gentle reminders to assure that the action items were actually performed.

After the follow-up was complete, we held a review telecon with the GC and the head of the Squire Sanders team. Interestingly, the GC chose to attend that meeting in person at Squire Sanders' office. He was there to follow up on a variety of joint actions, including several that had grown out of the workshop.

Of course, clients and their law firms have always collaborated, but never before in such a structured and efficient fashion. This workshop increased client satisfaction and collaboration efficiency and took the relationship to a new level. It helped integrate law firm services with client operations to deliver greater value to them.

Were there any problems? In my opinion, there was one big one: The participants simply could not find enough time to reap all the benefits of LPM. That challenge began the day the client agreed to the program and continued to the day it ended. It took several months to find a date when these extremely busy lawyers could all meet in the same room for the workshop, and in the follow-up period deadlines sometimes had to be adjusted due to other more pressing matters.

I was reminded of a series of posts that ran in the Association of Corporate Counsel blog a while ago that advised to "Follow the promise and pitfalls of forming a new value-based client-firm relationship." In Part 16 of the series Ken Grady, GC at Wolverine Worldwide, described the benefits of a program with Seyfarth, but then said, "What did we not do well? It took too long... General counsel of small legal departments often… get pulled in a lot of directions with little real control over their schedule."[94]

The fact that lawyers are busy is not exactly headline news. But lawyers, law firms, and their clients must find a way to collaborate, despite these barriers.

As Seyfarth Chairman, Steve Poor, has noted:

> Much of what we've done is most effective when deployed in a collaborative change process with clients. What we overlooked at the outset is that, by and large, our clients are lawyers, too, and many of them are the products of the culture of their own business… The nature of the process requires a continuous, but slow march toward improvement and adaptation. Some things we tried worked and some did not. Nevertheless, the continuous move forward takes persistence and, perhaps, a bit of stubbornness.[95]

Williams Mullen: Just-in-time training plus a course

Williams Mullen, a 240-lawyer firm in North Carolina, Virginia, and Washington DC, provides an example of how the just-in-time training approach works.

The good news is that if you do it right, legal project management produces measurable benefits and develops its own momentum. The bad news is that change takes time, especially the kind of fundamental change that LPM ultimately involves.

We held the kickoff meeting for our first just-in-time training workshop at Williams Mullen in October 2010. The participants were three of their top litigators and three of their top transactional lawyers. In the workshop, each lawyer identified an LPM action item that could benefit their practice, and then a coach followed up with them for 30 days to maximize results.

Williams Mullen was so pleased with the results that they decided to schedule another session right away. As it turned out, "right away" meant four months, because that's how long it took to find a date that worked well for another six lawyers. That second group achieved even more. Then Williams Mullen got enthusiastic about rolling out a larger program that included more traditional training.

Again, the goal was to rush. But given law firm dynamics, programs like this inevitably take time to roll out. At Williams Mullen, a few key partners kept pushing forward, led by John Paris, chair of the firm's Innovation Committee. On several occasions when committees met, next steps were debated, dates slipped, and Paris apologized for the delays. When he did, I always thought to myself, "You should see how long other firms are taking."

Ten months after the second workshop, we offered our half-day "Introduction to Legal Project Management" workshop to about 35 of Williams Mullen's top rainmakers in their Richmond, Virginia office.

When we began preparing for the workshop, we had an unusual opportunity to go back and interview people who had participated in our just-in-time training eight to twelve months before.

Litigator Camden Webb stressed the marketing benefits of LPM: "The environment is tough out there and it's a lot harder to get cases than it used to be. But the one thing that clients perk up about is when we describe a managed fee approach: 'We're going to predict what it will cost you before we start, and then keep you informed as things develop.'"

In litigation, LPM often requires a phased approach. "I can tell you what it will cost to respond to the specific complaint, and then we can scope out the rest… We can see what the next 30 days will look like and then go from there."

Webb then cited several confidential examples of work Williams Mullen has gotten as a result of their emphasis on increased planning before cases begin, and aggressive management once they are underway.

He has also been developing standard tools and forms in order to "Take high-minded lawyer work and make it much more efficient." For example, research guides for particular types of cases can serve as training tools for associates and refreshers for partners.

When we presented our LPM workshop at Williams Mullen, the handouts included a five-page sample from Webb's toolkit (Checklist for Analyzing an Unfair and Deceptive Trade Practices Claim under N.C. Gen. Stat § 75-1.1, et seq). The handouts also included sample case plans that were developed from a checklist of questions to ask clients at the beginning of a case to define the scope and help determine what the most efficient team should look like.

Webb and his partners are creating a triage process for litigation. Templates, standard operating procedures, and forms are helping to make routine, repeatable work more efficient and to free up time for them to work on novel high-end cases.

On the transactional side of the house, M&A attorney Steve Burke has also seen LPM marketing benefits, especially in relation to alternative fee arrangements (AFAs).

Burke participated in Williams Mullen's second just-in-time workshop in March 2011. When I interviewed him eight months later, he mentioned that a client had recently called him with a question about possibly using an AFA. "I was able to answer the question in 15 minutes," Burke said. "Before our LPM training, that would have taken me much longer."

This is not to say that the workshop introduced Burke to LPM for the first time. One of the reasons he had been selected to participate in the class was that he had a reputation as a highly organized proponent of careful matter management. But before taking the class, Burke said, he always started project management later in the deal. Our just-in-time program enabled him to see that the sooner you start, the better off you are. Talking to the client more at the beginning and thinking clearly at the start about scope, fees, expectations, and how things will play out, makes an enormous difference in the way a matter is handled, instead of "Hitting the ball back and forth like a tennis match."

These skills are especially useful for fixed fee matters. Does that mean that fixed fees are a way to higher profits? Some legal experts certainly think so. We wish they were right, but we think that in today's highly competitive legal marketplace, a "win some, lose some" portfolio approach is more realistic at most firms.

That's why some AFA leaders prefer to bid on portfolios of cases rather than single matters. Writing in ACC's blog, Nicole Nehema Auerbach of Valorem put it this way:

> Pricing a portfolio of matters… is easier for us and better for the client because it allows us to spread the risk inherent with one case across more. This allows us to provide a lower overall fee since the risk of an outlier, a deviation from the norm, is diminished. It also allows us to customize the bonus on either a case-by-case basis or some achievement for the portfolio overall. For example, our bonus can be tied to the overall savings in

> litigation spend, or simply the amount of savings we achieved across the portfolio in connection with settlement or judgment payouts.[96]

Or, as Williams Mullen's Burke summed it up, "When you commit to billing on a fixed fee basis, you need to take the bad with the good and with a smile on your face."

When I asked Camden Webb to predict the future, he said that the greatest challenge will be figuring out how closely they can adhere to the eight issues in our LPM book when they are deep in the throes of a particular case. "It is a lot easier to define the initial scope than it is to stick to it. The discipline of project management is difficult, especially dealing with issues like, 'Yes, I do have to track my time, and yes, I do need to know how much has been spent at key milestones.'"

Transactional attorney Allison Domson spoke for the entire profession when she said, "Legal project management is a new mentality. It needs to be accepted, but it is going to take time."

Gray Plant Mooty: Just-in-time training

Gray Plant Mooty is a Minneapolis-based firm with more than 150 lawyers.

Their interest in LPM started when Mark Williamson, the co-chair of the M&A practice and a member of the firm's board of directors, attended a two-day Legal Service Management Workshop put on by the Association of Corporate Counsel. Williamson walked out of that session convinced that Gray Plant Mooty and its clients could substantially benefit from LPM, and began to plan how.

In September 2011, the firm began with a pilot test of our just-in-time training workshop. Six participants, including Williamson, applied our identified action items, and a coach then followed up with each of the six for 30 days to assure success.

Williamson's action items revolved around creating an annual action plan for a fixed-fee regulatory program which included all of a public client's annual SEC filings, as well as producing and circulating minutes for board and board committee meetings. The effort involved creating a master schedule, task assignments, time allocations, and budget estimates. Among other things, he used simple tools already available in Outlook to create and share calendars, schedule meetings, and set internal lawyer team and external client reminders.

The results convinced Williamson and key partners that both clients and the firm could benefit if he expanded the approach to a variety of types of deals. Since then, M&A has become one of the most active practice groups in applying LPM in the firm. After the initial program was completed, he began developing and refining systematic processes to improve initial fee estimates and cost structures by breaking down complex matters into smaller tasks, planning and tracking the time spent on each task, and communicating better internally.

His group became particularly interested in using task codes to budget, plan, track, and manage the work, and began using their new knowledge to offer clients innovative fee structures as alternatives to traditional hourly billing. "It's being talked about more and more," Williamson said. "We are increasingly using these techniques on deals, and even lawyers who were skeptical initially are starting to use them."

According to the firm's Executive Director Karen Reynolds, one of the reasons the first pilot test was so successful was that the firm's new Finance Director, Shelbie O'Brien, was one of the six participants in the initial training. Like many great ideas, this happened by accident. The day before the first video workshop, one of the six lawyers who was scheduled to participate dropped out due to a last minute demand on her time, and O'Brien took her place. O'Brien decided to focus on improving the use of the tools and reports already available in the firm's financial software (Aderant) to help lawyers plan and manage budgets.

"Having Shelbie as part of the project management team means that she is actively involved on a daily basis in supporting the initiatives that developed as a result of the training," said Reynolds. "To cite just one example, Shelbie and her finance staff are now working in a partnership with two attorneys in our Business Advisory Group and our IT staff to develop templates to gather information for AFAs and make it quicker and easier to create engagement letters for a variety of AFAs."

Based on the success of the first just-in-time training workshop, the firm completed two more over the next nine months.

The expansion of the program highlighted the need to plan an LPM Sustainability Initiative to produce follow-up plans targeting each of the firm's practice areas, in order to ensure the specific, actionable, and efficient use of attorney time, bring about the continued sharing of best practices among attorneys, and provide accountability to keep the LPM momentum moving. "We didn't want legal project management to be something that we trained for, and then put on the shelf," Reynolds explained. "We wanted a way to continue the momentum, to drive this into firm culture without having to pay consultants on a continuing basis."

When the first just-in-time program was finished, Reynolds and Williamson began by holding monthly meetings in which the six participants talked about how to "spread [their] knowledge base." When they added six more from the second workshop group, the meetings became harder to schedule and to run. Reynolds and I then brainstormed alternatives and decided to break the large group down into several smaller monthly meetings of just two or three key people who shared common interests and goals.

Reynolds now meets once a month with each small group to talk about their projects, discuss the outcomes of their LPM work, and review the resources that they need. The core members of each group bring selected other attorneys, including associates, into the project management work, in order to spread the knowledge base. Reynolds "connects the dots" between the groups and avoids overburdening the attorneys with long discussions that don't relate to their practice areas. She also holds occasional meetings of all LPM participants so that everyone can be informed in a broad sense about what's going on.

Gradually, LPM is being woven into the fabric of the way that the firm serves its clients. When we trained the second and third groups, we were excited to note that each group seemed more motivated than the one before, and that the action items they identified were increasingly sophisticated. Very simply, best practices spread because Gray Plant Mooty lawyers and their clients rapidly saw the benefits.

Of the practice groups that have made the most progress, the labor and employment group is near the top of the chart. In all honesty, this has been surprising to firm insiders, including Judy Langevin, the senior partner who has led the labor and employment effort.

When we interviewed Langevin before the first workshop, she discussed her skepticism about the program and about LPM. Due to a last-minute work conflict, she was forced to drop out of the first program the day before the video workshop.

But Langevin signed up for the second workshop and ended up becoming one of LPM's strongest supporters. Her action items involved developing documents based on project management principles that can be used in their daily client work. Specifically, she created templates to streamline wage and hour compliance programs. She developed a prototype statement of work, a work breakdown structure, and sample budgets for use in planning, staffing, and pricing the work. This ultimately led to a document that outlines the procedures for conducting a review of an employer's classification of employees and compliance with federal wage/hour laws. It lists the types of information that the lawyers normally collect from the client and the factors affecting the fees to be charged.

After the program was complete, Langevin and her partners continued to create other templates, including one for estimating the costs of a litigation matter from the initial response to a lawsuit through the end of trial, with provisions for high and low estimates depending on the nature of the litigation. Additional compliance review templates have been developed for labor law, executive compensation, independent contractor review, social media and technology risk, 401(k) review, I-9 compliance, internships, retirement plan governance, background checks and application screening, and group health plans.

As a result of this experience, Langevin came to believe that the process of LPM is not some deep dark secret to be mastered by a select few, but rather a systematic and disciplined application of best practices from law firm and business management.

"What LPM is really all about is to have the right people doing the right work at the right time, to increase client value," said Langevin. "It includes clear communication with clients about what makes up the tasks that a lawyer does. This became an excellent vehicle to get us to talk with our clients about our work, which is something we should be doing anyway. It's a great way to tell clients, 'Here's what we can predict and control in your matters, and here's what it will cost.'"

Langevin is now an active participant in the firm's monthly LPM Sustainability Initiative meetings. In addition, she asked each of the 12 members of her practice group to come to a recent retreat with at least one concrete idea on how to use legal project management in their practice.

"We are introducing these concepts into the fabric of what we do," Langevin said. "Perhaps this is somewhat slower than what some aficionados would prefer, but we want all the attorneys to feel good about it. If we try to shove it down people's throats, it's not going to work."

She does not tell other attorneys at the firm, "Go find a project, then manage it." Rather, she asks them, "What do you do on a regular basis that can help you be more efficient for a client? "This way, she says, project management "sounds less like a buzzword, and more a matter of simply doing a better job of what we're already doing."

None of these activities are rocket science. The hardest part of LPM is getting lawyers started.

Langevin has changed from a skeptic to a believer, and says that as a result of this experience, "Legal project management has fundamentally changed the way I practice law."

Bilzin Sumberg: Just-in-time coaching

"Legal project management demands a new way of thinking about providing legal services," according to Al Dotson, a member of the Executive Committee at Bilzin Sumberg and the practice group leader of its Government Relations and Land Development Practice Group. "Before I started on our firm's LPM initiative, I approached new client engagements with a simple thought: 'You, the client, have engaged me. My hourly rate is X,' and that was the end of the discussion. Now I approach new engagements more in terms of developing a mutual understanding with the client about the services we will provide, the time it will take, the team required, the budget, and the relevant reporting milestones."

Dotson explained these ideas when I conducted a panel discussion with him, Jon Chassen, and Mitch Widom at Bilzin's annual partner retreat in March 2012. All three partners had just finished a pilot test of LPM coaching. For about three months, each lawyer had selected real world matters to analyze and identified the key issues that were most critical in each situation, using the templates, job aids and checklists in our *Legal Project Management Quick Reference Guide*. Then they reviewed the best practices described in the book and discussed exactly how to apply them to increase client value and protect profitability.

At the retreat, all three reported benefits, but Dotson's remarks got the most attention because his LPM activities had already led to new business in just a few short months. Dotson represents real estate developers and contractors in highly complex matters that involve a series of government regulatory agency approvals, and his developer clients loved the approach because they use project management to run their own businesses. One of them was so impressed by the legal project plan Dotson had produced that he asked Bilzin to take on a significant amount of new work.

The reason Dotson first volunteered for the program was that he "was looking for better ways to organize my work, and to respond to clients' and prospective clients' desires for budgets. Clients are looking for a way in which I can describe the work in advance, both in terms of what the cost of the whole engagement will be, and in terms of manageable segments of work."

Dotson described the LPM coaching he received as "spot-on" in that it helped him organize his complex matters in terms of their component parts, and to plan better for possible contingencies that may occur. "This coaching was far from a theoretical exercise," he said. "This was a discussion of specific matters that were before me, and how to approach them."

In weekly telephone sessions of about 30 minutes each, our coach walked Dotson through key problems and issues that he was encountering in his practice, and how best practices from other firms might apply. Dotson then followed up by completing written assignments based on our coaching materials and the existing project management literature.

As Dotson summed it up, "This coaching has been very beneficial to me in client management and in client development. I believe that it applies to all areas of law."

Bilzin Sumberg is a Florida-based firm of about 100 lawyers with, according to its web page, "A local footprint, a national presence and a global perspective." As a result of the discussion at the retreat, a number of other partners became interested in discussing how LPM could help them.

All 51 partners were offered the option to complete the same three-month coaching program that Dotson, Chassen, and Widom had received. Eight people signed up right after the retreat. Based on their results, another 14 signed up in September, for a total of 25 partners in the program to date, representing almost half of the firm's partners.

While we have seen lawyers from many firms make progress on LPM using a variety of approaches, we believe Bilzin Sumberg has made more LPM progress more quickly than any other law firm. The reason is very simple: they have the highest percentage of partners who have made a commitment to an intensive three-month coaching program. (We work with one AmLaw 100 firm that has put more total lawyers through this program, but because they are so much larger, their percentage is lower.)

Many firms have offered one-time training classes to a large number of lawyers, and a few have spent years in intensive re-engineering of business processes. But as far as we have been able to determine, no other firm on the planet has gotten such a large percentage of the partnership actively involved so quickly in making immediate changes that benefit their clients and their business.

The intensive LPM coaching approach works because each lawyer focuses on immediate ways to directly benefit their individual practice. And when it works, they tell their colleagues.

Litigation partner Scott Wagner was one of the first lawyers to volunteer for LPM coaching after the retreat presentation. Although Wagner usually represents defendants in antitrust cases and other types of complex litigation, he is now spending a good deal of his time representing plaintiffs in a huge civil antitrust case pending in the Northern District of California.

Wagner's clients are distributors and purchasers of products containing LCD screens. The background is that manufacturers of LCD screens were criminally charged with price-fixing and some were ultimately convicted. In cases like these, purchasers and others who suffered financial injury from the price-fixing conspiracy often sue the alleged conspirators for damages.

"When I signed up for the LPM coaching, I wanted to think about what I could do to get better in budgeting time and money for each case," Wagner said. "To some extent, this sounds like simple math, but figuring out the whole universe of tasks isn't easy."

One good example was accounting for the time that he and his team spent in daily monitoring of the criminal antitrust trial. "This is time that we had to budget, but it is also time that we wouldn't normally think about," Wagner said. "What my coach helped me to do was to think through, in advance, all the phases of a case, all the possible twists and turns and the directions it can take."

The result, Wagner said, was that he became much better at "giving the internal team and clients a more realistic estimate of what a case will cost." He is now able to estimate how much time—and money—a case will require under various assumptions.

In addition, he said, the legal project management process can help plan the staffing of a case. "Perhaps instead of two associates assigned, you may find that you need just one, or maybe three or four."

"The biggest take-away," Wagner continued, "is that budgeting is possible. The conventional wisdom is that it is not possible in litigation. But actually, you can come up with a budget that is useful to your client and can lay out all the contingencies to know what the litigation will likely cost."

These new skills had a significant impact on Wagner's practice after the coaching was concluded. For example, he reported, "In one case, we were approached about a plaintiffs' side antitrust action with a contingency fee arrangement. I was able to use my new budgeting techniques to better project the amount of time and resources it would take for us to see the matter through to completion. This gave us a much better springboard from which to analyze whether the matter was worth the firm's risk."

For Alan D. Axelrod, chair of the firm's Corporate and Securities Group, LPM training is all about looking at the law firm as a business. "I think that in the 80s and 90s people didn't look at law firms as businesses, but everyone got a rude awakening in the last few years.

"From a project management viewpoint, you must develop skills to make sure that work is not duplicated. You always needed to get the deal done as quickly and effectively as possible. But now you also have to think about getting the deal done efficiently," Axelrod said. "There is often a balancing required between the goal of completing it as soon as possible and still being as efficient as possible."

More and more clients are requesting caps, estimates, and similar fee arrangements for M&A and other transactional work, Axelrod said. "One client whom I had worked with many years ago is now back and growing its business. We just did an M&A deal for them where we carved out the due diligence aspect on an hourly basis and came up with a flat number for all the rest of it, in the form of a cap. If it comes in lower, we told them, 'We'll bill you for whatever it is.'"

Another transaction he's been working on was cleared by the SEC during the coaching and came in within budget. "In this one, we were aggressive in terms of the fixed fee number that we bid." Although Bilzin already had committed to the price before the coaching started, the coaching was still useful, and "It was very important to develop the template to help monitor the actual versus projected cost.

"The program was helpful, and as we get more and more experienced with LPM, it will become even more helpful," Axelrod said.

"The bottom line is the legal business has become so much more competitive—clients are looking for value and recognizing that the required work needs to be correlated with cost. If you don't move with the times, you'll be in trouble. LPM is one of the key tools for keeping up."

Another lawyer who went through the program was Real Estate Practice Group Leader Jim Shindell, who said, "We have always thought that we need to be efficient, but LPM coaching has given us a much better understanding of how to get there and what interferes with efficiency in a transaction. We were reactive in the past. Now we are becoming more proactive."

In his weekly 30-minute coaching calls, Shindell said, "We worked on ways to help us manage transactions to be efficient, to price matters more effectively, and to think a project out well ahead of time in order to staff it properly."

Many of the calls involved looking back at historical transactions (with some of the facts changed to ensure client confidentiality), and re-engineering the transactions to see how they might be done differently if they were new projects.

"We are looking to develop templates to help us identify all the tasks required in advance for any project so that we are not reinventing the wheel every time that we put out a price estimate," Shindell said.

The idea is "To break each transaction into the smallest possible parts, and then to re-imagine the transaction and all that it requires."

The resulting templates and checklists offer many benefits to clients, including an early identification of key steps in a transaction. They also offer the best way to predict what transactions will cost, Shindell said, so that no one is making things up by extrapolation or merely using wishful thinking. In time, Bilzin plans to refine the task codes it uses to track costs and analyze the historical record of how long things take under a variety of conditions. But clients can't wait, and templates and checklists provide a great way of offering more accurate estimates today.

"The idea is to be able to establish meaningful cost estimates, in advance, for our clients in the transactional matters that we handle," Shindell explained. The process of making a time investment up front through better planning and analysis actually saves time in the long run by permitting the firm to respond quickly and accurately to client requests for quotations.

Things move fast in the world of real estate. When a project is ready, the developer wants it to start immediately, and time is money. If we can move quickly with a cost estimate, Shindell said, that is a service both for our clients and for ourselves, and "That is why we are working so hard to develop the firm's institutional knowledge and collective data base."

In the current highly competitive environment, Shindell said, "If you're not able to properly and quickly determine your prospective costs in a matter, you will find yourself losing certain business, or perhaps not even being able to compete for business. And that includes a lot of good, highly sought real estate development business, not just business where the key determinant is price."

In general, when it comes to LPM, "As a firm we have made significant progress, but we still have a long way to go. The firm's leaders are squarely behind LPM, and just about everyone thinks it's a good idea. But it's a lot easier to say it than to do it."

Chapter 6
Pricing theory

If you are the kind of person who wants to understand the issues that lie behind changes in legal pricing, this chapter is for you. Others may prefer to skim the highlights, or jump ahead to the real world implications in Chapter 7: "How law firms are changing their pricing."

In 2009, a senior partner in our *LegalBizDev Survey of Alternative Fees* predicted, "Some law firms are going to large companies and offering to do all their legal work for one fixed price, but the firms don't know how it will work out in the long run. I suspect in some cases it will come out really ugly."[97]

In the years since, this prediction has become a reality and many fixed price legal deals have indeed turned out badly. We can expect more of this in the future, especially if firms continue to engage in the kind of "suicide pricing" described in Chapter 1 and in Bruce MacEwen's blog post series "Growth is Dead."[98]

In the *2012 Law Firms in Transition Survey*, Altman Weil asked managing partners and chairs, "Compared to projects billed at an hourly rate, are your firm's non-hourly projects more profitable or less profitable?"[99] Twenty-nine percent said non-hourly matters were less profitable.

Of these 29%, there is no data on how many turned out "really ugly." But based on many stories I have heard off the record, I would guess quite a few. I also suspect that the true number of less profitable deals is much higher than 29%.

In college, I had a friend who spent a lot of time at the racetrack. He seemed to remember the times he won much better than the times he lost. I suspect many lawyers have a similar talent for forgetting deals that turned out badly. Especially when they answer questions in a survey.

Of the other respondents in the Altman Weil survey, 14% said non-hourly arrangements were more profitable, and 40% said they were about the same as hourly. The remaining 17% were "not sure."

Some financial systems were set up for a simpler world of hourly billing, and firms with these systems did not know whether they were making money or losing money on AFAs. Legal software vendors have been scrambling to update their systems, and in the four years that Altman Weil has been asking this question, the percentage of firms who were unsure has been going down. But the fact that in 2012 17% of firms still didn't know whether their multi-million dollar AFAs were making money or losing it shows how much work law firms still have to do to adapt to this new world.

Would you invest in a company that didn't know which deals were profitable? Of course not. But if you are a partner in a large or mid-sized firm, there's a 17% chance you already own one.

How did this happen?

The answer can be traced to too many years of good news. For the last few decades, the law firm pricing model could be described as "cost plus a lot." Just keep raising prices until the overhead is paid and key partners make a lot of money. But now the game is changing, and clients are resisting rate increases.

Very simply, clients are demanding more value for their legal dollar, and that is not about to change, no matter what happens to the economy.

Going forward, when law firms offer non-hourly AFAs, they must address two fundamental questions:

1. When bidding for new work, how do I set a price that is high enough to protect profits, but low enough to get the work?
2. After winning the work, how do I manage the matter so that I make a profit (or at least break even) at that price?

Answering these questions will require lawyers to develop many new skills, including project management to deliver high quality legal services within limited budgets, and better bidding in the first place.

For the average partner, learning more about pricing must start with a very simple insight. As Bruce Clearing Sky Christensen, Executive Director of Warner Norcross & Judd put it, "Lawyers must understand that client perceptions of value may have nothing to do with the hours it takes to do the work."

But don't feel bad; lawyers are not the only ones who could be better at pricing. In the fifth edition of *The Strategy and Tactics of Pricing*, one of the most widely respected texts in this field, Thomas Nagle, John Hogan and Joseph Zale noted that, "In many business-to-business markets, where high-volume repeat purchasers negotiate their purchases, buyers are ahead of sellers in thinking strategically.... Buyers have goals and a long-term strategy for driving down acquisition costs, while suppliers rarely have comparable long-term strategies for raising or at least preserving margins."[100]

Wikipedia lists 21 different pricing strategies suppliers use in other businesses, ranging from loss leaders to premium pricing. Two of them are of special interest to lawyers: cost-plus and value pricing.

Cost-plus pricing is similar to the traditional hourly billing approach, and is exactly what it sounds like: a price is based on the cost of delivering a service plus a markup or profit margin. But that is much harder than it sounds, and not necessarily a good idea.

The most popular alternatives are built around the idea of *value pricing*, where the client's perception of value is the most important factor. The best-known proponent of this approach is Ron Baker, author of several books on the topic. In practice, this too can be harder than it sounds.

In a highly competitive marketplace like legal services, where some firms these days seem downright desperate for new work, there is also a giant wild card: price competition.

The legal profession is changing rapidly, and law firms are just starting to develop new approaches to pricing, so there is controversy about what will work best. This is further complicated by the rising popularity of several types of AFAs, as explained in Chapter 9. But on one point everyone can agree: law firms could make more money if they got better at setting their prices.

The cost-plus approach

After I gave a speech at the retreat of a 1,000-lawyer firm, a senior partner once asked, “In your experience, how do large firms determine costs?” I replied, “Mostly, they don’t. Until recently, most firms were making so much money they didn’t need to precisely calculate their costs.”

Some firms are sophisticated in their cost analysis, but many lawyers seem to think of their standard hourly rates as being equal to the firm’s costs. But traditionally, rates have actually been based on “cost plus a lot,” and no one was quite sure which part was the cost and which part was the “plus a lot.”

To review the basic concepts, let’s start with the simplest possible example: a single-lawyer firm. Multiply by 500 and add complex interactions and you will begin to get the picture for a 500-lawyer firm.

Our hypothetical case describes some pricing calculations for Beth, an AmLaw 200 senior associate who specializes in labor law and is considering going out on her own.

Last year Beth billed 2,000 hours at an average rate of $300 per hour. Since the firm charged $600,000 for her time, and Beth was paid a salary of $250,000, the firm’s share of her billings was $350,000. It seems obvious to Beth that if she hung her own shingle, she should be able to charge less and make more.

Since Beth plans to bill by the hour, her first question is what she should charge per hour. She expects to bill 2,000 hours in her first year, and would like to get started by at least keeping her $250,000 salary as a base. She has done a business plan and anticipates overhead of $100,000. Thus her basic earnings requirement is a total of $350,000 to cover her overhead of $100,000 and required salary of $250,000.

As summarized in this table, some simple math tells Beth that she can bill 2,000 hours at an average rate of $200 per hour, bring in $400,000 in revenue, and make a profit beyond the $350,000 base expense.

Description	Budget
Salary	$250,000
Realized Hours	2,000
Overhead	$100,000
Salary + Overhead = Expense	$350,000
Hourly Billing Rate	$200
Total Revenue	$400,000
Profit	$50,000

Profit was calculated by multiplying the hourly billing rate by the total number of hours billed and subtracting salary and overhead. This profit is the "plus" in cost-plus.

Beth requires a salary of $250,000 for herself and considers this a cost of doing business. She wants to ultimately make more than she did in her old job, and this is the reason for the planned profit of $50,000.

When her profit is 0, she breaks even. In this example, it is easy to find the billing rate at which she breaks even: just divide the base expense by the number of billable hours planned.

Breakeven billing rate =

$$\frac{\$350{,}000 \text{ expenses}}{2{,}000 \text{ billable hours}} = \$175 \text{ per hour}$$

The break-even billing rate of $175 represents the hourly cost of meeting her overhead and planned salary. Her actual rate of $200 per hour has added in an extra $25 per hour to achieve the desired profit. This is Beth's cost-plus model.

But even in this very simple situation, there is a problem: the numbers above are planning numbers. What Beth will actually make cannot be determined until the end of the year when she looks back at what actually happened. It is very unlikely that her prediction of the future will be exactly right. It could be very wrong.

Suppose that in the first year Beth actually has overhead of $90,000 but is only able to bill for 1,800 hours. Her results would look like this:

Description	Projected	Actual
Salary	$250,000	$250,000
Overhead	$100,000	$90,000
Total Expense	$350,000	$340,000
Realized Hours	2,000	1,800
Actual Hourly Rate	200	200
Total Revenue	$400,000	$360,000
Profit	$50,000	$20,000

Beth's actual break-even rate was higher than planned—it was $340,000 expenses / 1,800 billable hours = $188.89. If she had been able to bill only 1,000 hours, and paid herself the same salary, it would have been $340 per hour ($340,000 expenses / 1,000 billable hours).

These numbers can be very important. Suppose that Beth is asked to compete for work on a matter by lowering her hourly billing rate. Unless she is desperate for new work and willing to lower her salary, the lowest hourly rate she quotes should be her breakeven rate—the amount she needs to charge to cover overhead and salary.

But, as suggested by this example, the breakeven rate cannot be known for certain until year-end. Hourly billing seems easy when there is plenty of work and little price pressure, but when competition gets tougher it can be difficult to figure out just how much you can lower prices and still break even.

In the legal profession, there is also a great deal of confusion about what it means to break even, and where profit begins.

We have used the word "profit" in its standard business sense—the amount that is left after expenses and required salaries are paid. Unfortunately, the term "partner profit" is not typically used in this way in the legal profession. Partner profit usually refers to the amount of cash remaining to distribute to equity partners after all other expenses and *non-partner salaries* are paid. Partner salaries come out of the "partner profits" pool.

In a large firm, if there were no partner profits, partners would be paid nothing for their work. If clients read in the *American Lawyer* that 2012 partner profits were 38%, they may be irritated at the excess if they don't stop and think that this so-called profit actually includes the basic amount that the partners live on.[101] For a detailed analysis of the problems this can cause, see the section on the "Litigation investment model" in the next chapter.

To cite an extreme example of the difficulty of defining break-even in the legal profession, consider Wachtell, Lipton, Rosen & Katz, which had the highest profits per partner in the AmLaw 100 in 2012: $4.46 million.[102] Some equity partners were paid more than this average, some were paid less. But let's consider a lawyer who was paid exactly that amount. He may think of his $4.46 million annual draw as a cost of doing business. But the chances are Wachtell Lipton could stay in business if he were forced to scrape by on $3 million per year, or even $2 million. What fraction of his draw is a true cost and what part is his share of the profits? Until the day that Wachtell Lipton guarantees equity partners a baseline salary, and identifies the rest as a discretionary profit-sharing bonus, the line between cost and plus will remain arbitrary.

At large and mid-sized firms, few if any lawyers could tell you what their break-even rate was, which can make it hard to know how little they should be willing to bid in a competitive marketplace.

If that were not complicated enough, in a sophisticated financial model one could assume that different practice groups have different overhead rates. Perhaps one practice group needs an impressive office and high entertainment expenses to succeed, while another could be successful in more modest offices with limited client entertainment. That would imply that the high spending lawyers would be assigned a higher overhead rate, and when times got tough, their practice group would be the first to be squeezed. I would not want to be at the partner meeting where those figures got debated.

Despite these problems, most law firm pricing has traditionally been based on the cost-plus model. As Ron Baker points out in his influential book, *Pricing on Purpose*, it seems fair to start from costs and add a reasonable markup for profit. But Baker strongly favors the alternative of value pricing over cost-plus. After listing numerous bullet points that people use to argue in favor of the cost-plus approach, and explaining how they are wrong, he noted, "It is amazing how many businesses still cling to the cost-plus pricing method…. Doing something stupid once is just stupid. Doing it twice is a philosophy."[103]

The authors of *The Strategy and Tactics of Pricing* were a bit gentler when they said, "Cost-plus pricing is… in theory, a simple guide to profitability; in practice, it is a blueprint for mediocre financial performance. The problem with cost-driven pricing is fundamental: In most industries it is impossible to determine a product's unit cost before determining its price. Why? Because unit costs change with volume."[104]

In traditional legal work, the "unit" you are selling is the billable hour. We have seen that until you get to the end of a year and know exactly how many hours you have billed and been paid for, and how much you spent on everything else, you can only estimate the cost per hour, and your initial estimate will almost always be wrong. Maybe by a little and maybe by a lot.

Now take the uncertainties for a single lawyer, and multiply them by 100 lawyers or 1,000, with laterals coming and going, and client needs constantly changing, and you will begin to get an appreciation for how difficult it would be to accurately predict the cost per hour for a large firm at the beginning of the year. Any cost estimate at the beginning of the year will depend on a number of assumptions. And when some of those assumptions inevitably turn out to be incorrect, the cost numbers will change.

However, that is not to say it is impossible to estimate costs in advance. Government contractors who work under cost-plus contracts are required to estimate their costs at the beginning of each year, bill the government all year long at the estimated rate, and then do a reconciliation at the end of the year to determine actual reimbursable costs. If actual costs exceed the original estimate, contractors typically must request permission to exceed the contract estimate, giving the government 90 days advance notice. If costs are lower than the original estimate, at the end of the year the government gets a refund.

To make money within these rules, contractors set up elaborate financial reporting systems to provide early warning of variance from their projections, and they change their spending at the first sign of a problem. So it is certainly possible to run a company within narrow cost limits, but it requires a degree of financial analysis and control that would be a revolutionary change for law firms.

The result of all this is that many partners in large firms do not understand even the rough costs of each billable hour. Does it matter? Yes, it does. As one AmLaw 100 decision maker put it in the *LegalBizDev Survey of Alternative Fees*:

> Our partners are the salesmen as well as the producing managers on a lot of this work, so they've got to be armed with our own internal costs and how we can adjust those internal costs. If somebody comes back and says [that they'd] like to do this work, and [they know] what [they] need, but [that they] can only get $150,000 for the project, then we have to say [whether we can make it work, or] if we're doing it with no profit margin or as a loss leader. There need to be people in the organization that can sit down with the partners and talk to them about costs and [then] arm them to talk to the general counsels.[105]

Some CFOs, managing partners and other law firm leaders have a much better understanding of where their break-even point is than the typical partner does. In order to define that break-even point, they had to make some assumptions about the minimum acceptable compensation for each partner. You can probably understand why this analysis is often done behind closed doors, and the results remain confidential.

Cost-plus may or may not be a good basis for setting prices. But if law firms want to stay in business in an ever-more competitive world, they must ultimately charge at least as much as they spend. And that starts with understanding their costs.

Using cost information to estimate prices

After a lawyer has set an hourly rate that exceeds their break-even point, there is another obvious step required to set a fixed price or the budget for an hourly matter: you must determine the number of hours the matter will take.

It is very easy to do the math that says if a lawyer bills $300 per hour, and a matter will require 50 hours, the cost will be $15,000. But it can be very hard to come up with that estimate of 50 hours. When this calculation is the basis for quoting an estimate on hourly work, many lawyers are comfortable with a rough quote. This is risky, because estimates can quickly become what the client expects and thus a psychological price ceiling. And if the calculation is the basis for a fixed price bid, that should definitely get the lawyer's attention, since any costs past $15,000 will come out of her own pocket.

One way to reduce the risk of a fixed fee is to handle many of them, so that there will be winners to balance out the losers.

In stock portfolios, diversification helps to mitigate risk. With a wide selection of stocks, excess losses from a few unexpected losers can be offset by excess gains from a few unexpected big winners. The principle of diversification is a key component of modern portfolio theory in finance. The same principle can be applied to a group of legal matters.

Suppose the lawyer were in a position to bid on five similar 50-hour matters rather than just one. The results might look like this:

Matter	Hours Budgeted	Actual Hours
1	50	51
2	50	48
3	50	47
4	50	55
5	50	46
Total	250	247

In this example, efficiency increased over time, with the exception of matter 4, where some problem slowed things down. The individual matters 1 and 4 would be losers if they were handled alone, but with a portfolio approach, the total hours were actually lower than the fixed price bid. It is important to note that one of the benefits of handling a portfolio of similar matters from the same client is the possibility of learning from experience and improving efficiency with good project management.

This type of averaging is not some theoretical academic dream. It is what makes insurance possible. An actuary cannot predict the age when any single individual will die, but she can very accurately predict death rates for large groups of people, and use the information to set profitable rates for insurance.

For more complex matters involving a number of lawyers, a spreadsheet can be set up to calculate total costs based on the planned hours for each person working on the matter, multiplied by their hourly rate.

Of course, the more complex the matter, and the more people are involved, the harder it will be to estimate the required hours.

Many lawyers traditionally believed that it is simply not possible to predict the costs of complex legal matters. As the managing partner of a firm with more than 1,000 lawyers put it in *The LegalBizDev Survey of Alternative Fees*, "[Some] litigators say [a fixed fee] just doesn't work at all, because [no one] knows what's going to happen. You hear all those stories about how you can get a fixed fee to build the Taj Mahal. A litigator will say, well that's true, but when you're building the Taj Mahal, there isn't somebody who's paid to fend you off; in a contentious engagement, that's what's going on."

It's certainly true that the cost of defending a suit will be low if your opponent is willing to settle early in the process and high if they engage in scorched earth tactics. However, it is interesting to note that the senior partner quoted above manages a firm that has signed a number of highly publicized, multi-million-dollar deals to handle litigation for a fixed price. He went on to explain that success requires strong relationships, bidding one phase at a time rather than a single fee for the full matter, and a "win some, lose some" mentality.

Winning more often will require an improved ability to predict costs, and no one says that will be easy. No matter how good you get, some of your predictions will be wrong. But you can be right enough, often enough, to operate a profitable business.

This is an extremely important topic in a budget-conscious world, and many firms are currently developing procedures, forms, and templates to improve the budgeting process.

In addition, data mining of historical records is frequently used to understand the range of costs for different types of transactions and cases. Data mining sounds like a good idea, and many firms are investing a lot of time and money in this type of analysis. But data analysts warn of the risks of "garbage in, garbage out." The Association of Corporate Counsel's *Value-Based Fee Primer* notes that "Historical data will likely include… sub-optimal billing practices."[106] And if your database of historical costs is full of matters that were handled the old way with little attention to controlling costs, then it could be a waste of money to spend a lot of time analyzing that data.

After all these complications are addressed, and you come up with an hourly estimate, there is the strategic question of how to get from that estimate cost to a fixed price. You may think a matter will cost $15,000, but no one can be sure. So what should you charge to guarantee that price? Should you add a premium of 10% or 20% or more? The answer will depend not just on what you think is fair, but also on what clients are willing to pay.

Price competition, discounts, and loss leaders

"Law Firm Price Wars Break Out as Some Try 'Loss Leader' Bids for Work" said a November 2009 headline in the *ABA Journal*.[107] The article was based on the interviews I had conducted for the *LegalBizDev Survey of Alternative Fees* in which AmLaw 100 senior decision makers said things like: "It's a jungle out there."[108]

Since this piece appeared, in many markets legal price wars have evolved from front-page news to a way of life.

According to a recent survey of several thousand general counsel conducted by Acritas,[109] the number one reason GCs fired law firms was that they were too expensive.[110]

In a second survey published in the *American Lawyer*, 75% of law firm leaders said that more clients are requesting discounts, and 49% said clients are requesting deeper discounts.[111] In a separate survey conducted by Altman Weil, 90% of managing partners and chairs said that increasing price competition is not temporary, but rather a permanent change in the legal marketplace.[112]

In another survey conducted by ALM Legal Intelligence, 36% of 194 large law firms said they had been invited to participate in a reverse auction in which law firms are asked to propose a price for a particular service, and the lowest bid "wins" the work.[113] Three-quarters of those who were invited did bid, which represents a total of 27% of all law firms agreeing to reverse auctions. Talk about a race to the bottom.

The economic balance of power has shifted to clients. Just a few short years ago large law firms reigned supreme. Now it seems that almost all large corporations and their in-house counsel are asking for some sort of price break from their lawyers—even from firms they have used for decades. Many general counsel are seeing their legal budgets reduced, and they are passing the pressure along to their outside law firms.

In response, many firms are taking shortcuts to client satisfaction by offering discounts, and not paying enough attention to the way this reduces profits. This problem is familiar in other businesses, as noted in *The Strategy and Tactics of Pricing*. "Customer satisfaction can usually be bought by a combination of over delivering on value and underpricing products… The purpose of strategic pricing is to price more profitably by capturing more value, not necessarily by making more sales."[114]

Discounting can have a much bigger effect on profitability than you might think. For details, see the appendix for a discussion of formulas relating hourly discounts to profits, starting with an example in which a 10% discount reduced anticipated profits by 80%. The relationships are complex, but what seems like a small discount can sometimes have a very large impact on profits.

When law firms calculate their partner compensation these days, many are seeing all too clearly how discounting reduced their income much more than they expected.

Lawyers often justify discounts as loss leaders, under the theory that low prices will start a new relationship and later lead to more profitable work. But will it? Once clients become accustomed to low rates, it will be very difficult to get them to pay more.

If you do decide to use loss leaders to build new work, it might be wise to make sure the first job is a large one. A few years ago, Ron Paquette published an article in *Strategies: The Journal of Legal Marketing* describing research conducted by Redwood Analytics to evaluate the widely held idea that small jobs often grow into big clients:

> It's called the acorn theory—from a tiny seed of work in one legal area can grow a mature oak of a client, which provides work across many practices. Nice theory. But how often does it happen in practice? We thought this theory was largely a myth.... We've observed that regardless of the firm involved, most large clients appeared to have retained the firm for significant matters from the start of the relationship.[115]

So Paquette and his colleagues looked at the top five percent of clients at one AmLaw 100 firm and went back 23 years to see whether those clients had started large or small. More than 90% had started large (that is, already in the top 20% of the firm's clients in their very first engagement). When Paquette analyzed similar data from an AmLaw 200 firm, they again found that today's large clients had been large right from the start (in this case 84% of the clients). They concluded that, "Firms should be highly selective with regard to small clients. It is commonly held that small clients are on average less profitable than large clients. If your firm's growth strategy depends at all on growing small clients into larger and more profitable clients, think hard about the likelihood that this will happen."[116]

So what should law firms do? Some believe that the answer lies in an entirely different approach: value pricing.

Value pricing basics

Almost all law firms currently use the basic billable hour method with assorted variations on cost-plus pricing. But anyone who has ever heard of the ACC Value Challenge knows how important perceived value is to clients these days.

If you have thought about applying value pricing with your clients, you have probably read about the work of Ron Baker. His book, *Implementing Value Pricing: A Radical Business Model for Professional Firms*, provides an excellent overview of the theory of value pricing, and how it applies to accountants, lawyers, and other professional services firms.

As Baker defined it:

> The word value has a specific meaning in economics: "The maximum amount that a consumer would be willing to pay for an item." Therefore value pricing can be defined as the maximum amount a given customer is willing to pay for a particular service, before the work begins. This is not to suggest we can capture one hundred percent of maximum value, but rather that we have the potential to access some of it utilizing strategic pricing.[117]

Does that sound like price gouging? It's not. As Stanley Marcus (former president of Neiman Marcus), put it, "You're really not in business to make a profit, but you're in business to render a service that is so good people are willing to pay a profit in recognition of what you are doing for them."[118]

In cost-plus pricing, cost is known before you set the price. In value pricing, you start with the price the customer is willing to pay, then control your costs to meet that price. Baker summed up the difference in these two diagrams:

Cost-Plus Pricing

Services » Cost » Price » Value » Customers

Value Pricing

Customers » Value » Price » Cost » Services

Baker feels strongly that value pricing should replace hourly billing. His web page bio begins with this mission statement: "To, once and for all, bury the billable hour and timesheet in the professions." Chapter 17 of *Implementing Value Pricing* is titled "The Deleterious Effects of Hourly Billing" and describes numerous disadvantages, including misaligning interests, focusing on effort instead of results, hoarding of hours, leaving money on the table, and diminishing the quality of life. Chapter 18 explains why timesheets should be eliminated. Its title indicates the strength of Baker's feelings on this issue: "Why Carthage Must Be Destroyed."

Baker has also emphasized that value pricing can sometimes produce far more revenue than the hourly approach. He gave the example of an accounting firm that was engaged to develop an exit and management succession strategy which produced substantial tax savings. Initially the CPA billed at standard hourly rates, but at some point he said to the client, "I don't believe hourly rates [are]… appropriate [in this case]…. You tell me what all the value of this is to you…. I know I will be happy with whatever you come up with." Ultimately he was extremely happy because the total payment was "a little bit over $1 million."[119]

By then, he had stopped tracking time on this engagement, so it is impossible to say exactly how much he would have gotten on an hourly basis. However, he did say his prices had "skyrocketed" and reading between the lines our guess is that hourly rates would have totaled less than $100,000.

Any lawyer would love the concept of value pricing if it meant that she could get paid 10 times what she would earn for billing hours. And many law firms see value pricing as a ray of hope in a troubled marketplace, an opportunity to increase profitability at a time when there are unrelenting competitive pressures to charge less.

Baker noted that, "These types of engagements are certainly not the rule in any firm, they are the exception. Nonetheless, they do arise, and when they do it is critical to recognize the value you are creating and to utilize innovative pricing strategies to capture it."

Companies like Apple have become very profitable by creating consumer perceptions of value, and pricing products like the iPad and iPhone accordingly. But there is only one Apple, and there are dozens of companies like Dell, HP, Samsung, Lenovo, and Asus who find themselves competing on price.

A small number of the most profitable law firms in the world have been using value pricing for years, just as Apple has. But they are at the top of the profession and specialize in "bet the company" work. If a client is defending a multi-billion dollar lawsuit, or acquiring a powerful rival, or being accused of a white-collar crime, she will care much less about the price than about the outcome.

When Jim Durham published *The Essential Little Book of Great Lawyering*, he estimated such "bet the company" matters at only about 5% of all legal work. The rest he classified as important matters (65-70%) or commodity work (25-30%). After Durham published this book in 2005, all signs are that legal commodity work has grown, and "bet the company" and "important" work has shrunk.[120]

In my *Legal Business Development Quick Reference Guide*, I've written about the traditional marketing implications of these three different types of legal work, as summarized in the following table:

Type of legal work	Value's significance in marketing	Relationship's significance in marketing
Bet the company	High	Low
Important	Medium	High
Commodity	Low	Low[121]

The world is changing, and when it comes to getting new business, the marketing significance of providing value is going up, and the importance of prior relationships is going down.

The next section discusses the nuts and bolts of Ron Baker's eight steps to implementing value pricing. As we see it, the problem with value pricing is an expectations gap. Law firms want to believe value pricing will lead to higher prices and profits. Sometimes it can. But in most cases these days, when legal clients say "value" what they mean is "I need to pay you less."

Ron Baker's eight steps to implementing value pricing

The first four sections of Ron Baker's influential book, *Implementing Value Pricing: A Radical Business Model for Professional Firms*, review a number of interesting theories and arguments against hourly billing. But if you want to focus on the "how to," you can jump directly to Part V of his book, which describes Baker's "Eight steps to implementing value pricing."

Conversation. Talk to the client to determine her wants and needs. This requires genuine communication, so you must listen actively to understand what is on the client's mind.

Pricing the customer: Questions for the value council. Pricing is of such importance that Baker says each firm should have a value council that studies the results of the value conversation, and considers the best strategy for pricing each matter.

Developing and pricing options. The analysis in steps 1 and 2 can lead to an internal discussion of several different options to offer a client, at different price levels. According to Baker, this can help the client think about what is really of value for her and help the firm close a deal.

Presenting options to the customer. Then it is time to effectively present the options to the client, and address any objections.

Customer selection codified into the fixed price agreement. Baker assumes this conversation will lead to a fixed price agreement, which must be written carefully to "memorialize the meeting of the minds between the firm and the customer." Chapter 32 of his book includes a sample fixed price agreement.

Proper project management. Once the agreement is signed, the firm must manage the matter to live within the agreed-upon price.

Scope creep and change orders. In today's dynamic business environment, changes in requirements are almost inevitable. The firm and the client must have plans in place to decide when changes in scope lead to a change in price, and to resolve any problems or disagreements.

Pricing after action reviews. The US Army has a policy of after action reviews to evaluate missions after the fact and learn from what happened. This same type of retrospective review is helpful for setting future prices.[122]

Each of these eight steps is described in depth in its own chapter. For example, in the chapter on Step 1's conversation, Baker talked about:

> Twenty-seven questions you can ask your client.
>
> How to start the conversation and effectively point it in the right direction.
>
> How to listen carefully and hear what the client wants without dominating the conversation.
>
> How the firm should deal with clients who try to conceal information about how much your services are valued or what other firms may charge.
>
> How you should discuss risk with your clients.[123]

Similarly, Chapter 29 goes over the key elements of Step 2—what to do when you get back to the office and work on your pricing strategy based on that conversation. Again, there are long lists of useful tips.

For example, on page 245, there is a list of 16 items to consider in defining a good price, including:

> "Not allowing your dumbest competitors to set your price," which is related to the issue of avoiding price wars, as discussed previously.
>
> What questions should you ask yourself before setting the price? There is a list of 35 questions on page 247.
>
> Four types of buyers—price buyers, value buyers, convenience buyers and relationship buyers—and how to deal with each.
>
> What are the psychological factors that affect the price sensitivity of the client?[124]

Every lawyer can find valuable ideas and tools in this book, whether you agree with Baker's rejection of hourly billing or not.

However, you may question his optimism about what the market will bear for value pricing. In the section on "Dipping your toe into the water" for fixed pricing, Baker suggested calculating your initial fixed price estimate with a budget based on what you think your normal billable hours would be and then adding a premium of 50% to 90%.[125] That would be great way for law firms to do it, if they could find clients who were willing to pay 50% to 90% premiums in the current marketplace. A few firms may find such clients. But from what we've seen, most clients are looking to cut costs, and the firms that win fixed price deals these days often get no premium at all.

If you do decide to pursue value pricing, at some point you are going to have to just jump in.

In a post in his blog entitled "How to value price: Just do it," Baker advised lawyers to "Stop analyzing, stop looking for a checklist, a formula, or detailed instructions like this was a piece of IKEA furniture—there aren't any.... Just do it."[126]

Five ways to improve pricing

There is so much talk these days about value pricing and alternative fees that many people think of pricing simply as setting a fixed or alternative fee. However, you are pricing whenever you decide what to ask someone to pay for your services. When you set an hourly billing rate you are pricing, and when you discount that hourly rate, you are making a pricing decision.

Five basic ideas from the classic text *The Strategy and Tactics of Pricing* by Nagle et. al., now in its fifth edition, sum up this overview of pricing theory. These ideas can help any law firm to improve the way it sets prices:

1. ***Differentiate.*** You may have heard legal marketers use this word quite a bit, and it is just as important to pricing experts. According to *The Strategy and Tactics of Pricing*, "A product's total economic value is calculated as the price of the customer's best alternative (the reference value) plus the worth of whatever differentiates the offering from the alternative."[127] This differentiation value can be either monetary or psychological. Whatever features of a law firm add differentiating value, it is crucial that these features be communicated to the client. Are you different because your legal project management expertise makes you more efficient than others, or because you communicate progress better? Let the client know.
2. ***Communicate value.*** Value is perceived differently in different businesses. Legal services are difficult for clients to evaluate when compared to products like light bulbs or computers for which buyers can more easily get price and

performance information. "In our research, we have found that business managers rated 'communicating value and price' as the most important capability necessary to enable their pricing strategies."[128] They make special note of the value of an endorsement from a client known to be especially discriminating. For example, Kaiser Permanente has an excellent reputation for being an informed buyer in the health field. Thus "when other hospitals and health maintenance organizations (HMOs) learn that Kaiser Permanente has adopted a more expensive product or service, they assume that its price premium is cost-justified."[129]

3. ***Have a clear and consistent pricing policy.*** It is important to have a clear and consistent pricing policy and to avoid commonly granting price exceptions. We have already advised being cautious about discounting to win business because that creates client expectations of future discounts. *The Strategy and Tactics of Pricing* says that "Good policies lead customers to think about the purchase of your product as a price-value trade-off rather than as a game to win at your expense."[130] In setting up your policies it is important to keep in mind that people are more affected by perceived losses than perceived gains and you should frame your pricing with this in mind. If the client is offered a service package, it is better to have a policy that allows a reduction in cost if a service is dropped (a perceived gain) than a policy that requires an extra fee to get that service (a perceived loss).

4. ***Know your market segments.*** Clients are not all the same; they fall into different market segments. *The Strategy and Tactics of Pricing* gives an example of a company selling a scientific device to be used in DNA analysis. The device is a great improvement over existing competitor products, and the company estimated the differentiation value in order to set a price. However the company sold to two different market segments—the industrial market and the academic/government market. The differentiation value was

not the same in industry and universities, so the ultimate pricing strategy involved different pricing policies in the two segments. As long as this policy is clearly stated it does not violate consistency requirements. Airlines do this all the time when they distinguish between business travelers and nonrefundable touring seniors. What are your market segments?

5. ***Know your client types.*** Within a given market segment there may be different classes of clients, and knowing their classification may help you to deal more intelligently with each group. *The Strategy and Tactics of Pricing* divides clients into four categories:

   a. ***Value-driven clients*** have sophisticated analysis strategies for studying value added, and you will need to work to establish your value added for them.

   b. ***Brand buyers* are also known as *relationship buyers*.** For them, the cost of analyzing value added is perceived as too high. This "buyer will buy a brand that is well-known for delivering a good product with good service without considering cheaper but riskier alternatives."[131] This is an easier client so long as you do not disappoint her.

   c. ***Price buyers*** are looking for a specified service at the lowest possible price. Here you will need to "strip out any and every cost that is not required to meet the minimum specification."[132] It is also important to fence off this job, so that more lucrative clients who receive a higher level of service understand that this lower priced work is at a different level.

   d. ***Convenience buyers*** "don't compare prices; they just buy from the easiest source of supply."[133] They know that they are paying a premium for immediate convenience and will not complain.

Whether your pricing is based on value or cost-plus, and whether your typical agreements are hourly or AFAs, these general principles can help you set prices.

For more information on the challenges of setting prices and maintaining profits, see the Appendix "The mathematics of pricing."

Chapter 7
How law firms are changing their pricing

The last chapter reviewed the theory of pricing. This one provides a number of examples of what law firms are doing today to change the way they price legal matters.

One key factor that is driving the new pricing movement is the new emphasis on AFAs, and especially on fixed fees. As explained in Chapter 8, AFAs now account for more than 15% of all legal fee revenue. This figure is still small compared to the percent that is hourly, but it is measured in the billions, and all of the forces of change are headed toward more AFAs.

In the good old days of hourly arrangements with rates that went up every year, it did not require sophisticated financial analysis to send a bill that multiplied each lawyer's hourly rate by the number of hours spent. But to make AFAs profitable, law firms now need to spend more time thinking about pricing.

This is a rapidly changing area, and it will continue to evolve in coming years, with different firms finding different solutions depending on their needs and their culture.

The rise of the pricing function

The most famous pioneer in the alternative fee movement is Bartlit Beck Herman Palenchar & Scott, a Chicago firm of about 70 trial lawyers which *The American Lawyer* named "Litigation Boutique of the Year" in 2009. As their web page explains:

> Our approach to fees is unique, but simple. We believe our interests should be aligned with our clients'. To that end, we think we should get paid more if we win and less if we lose… We do not bill by the hour… We employ a variety of fee arrangements, including flat monthly fees, partial contingency fees, and similar alternatives… Our fees don't depend on how long we can spend on a task or how many associates we can put on it. Our fees depend on our success.[134]

Given the fact that they have completely rejected hourly billing, and that they have been succeeding at AFAs for much longer than most other law firms have known what AFA stands for, the obvious question is how they set prices. In 2009, I was on a West LegalEdcenter online panel with Fred Bartlit and asked him how they handled both pricing and project management.[135] Bartlit's answer was that both functions are completely centralized, and that there is no management committee at Bartlit Beck. "One guy, Skip Herman, runs the entire firm, from deciding which cases to accept to setting the price and staffing each matter. We have no firm meetings and no conferences; Skip runs everything."

Other firms have not gone this far, but a number of large firms are centralizing the pricing function in a variety of ways.

Stuart Dodds became Baker & McKenzie's first director of global pricing in 2011, after serving for three years as global head of pricing at Linklaters. His job includes four main components:

"We help **set** the price in a proposal, help **get** the price, help our fee earners **manage** the price through project management, and then **review** how effective the pricing approach taken has been on a long-term basis for both our client and our firm. We are building a whole infrastructure within the firm with pricing do's and don'ts."

Much of Dodds' time is focused initially on the firm's larger clients, and one key goal is to help ensure pricing consistency and rationality for a firm with 70 offices around the world and over 3,800 lawyers.

In April 2012, Toby Brown was hired by Akin Gump to serve as its first director of strategic pricing and analytics. He had previously filled a similar role at Vinson & Elkins, where the firm's leaders put out the word that whenever pricing is an issue with an important client, Brown should be consulted early and often.

One of the most important aspects of his job was to "create a culture of having conversations about value. Lawyers are really good at talking to clients about legal issues," said Brown. "Now, however, they need to add another dimension to the conversation to include value, pricing and efficiency.... Sometimes I think my job is almost 100% business development."

Others with related titles also emphasize how pricing is tied to client satisfaction and new business. Matt Laws, then senior manager of alternative fee arrangements and head of the pricing group at Reed Smith, said, "I see myself as working for the firm and for the client at the same time. I try to find that middle ground, a mutually beneficial arrangement."[136]

At this time a growing number of firms have a separate pricing director or department, and many see this as the wave of the future. "I find it hard to see how major firms could not organize themselves this way," said Michael Byrd, assistant director of pricing strategy and analysis at Mayer Brown. "What we do fits somewhere in-between finance and business development. It's at the same time both numbers-driven and creative."

Byrd sees the main benefit of a proactive pricing strategy as "increased competitiveness to keep us in the forefront of the market." Both Byrd and the partners he works with believe that the new emphasis on pricing has helped increase responsiveness to client needs, increase client satisfaction, and add value.

At Winston & Strawn in early 2012, the pricing strategy role was shared by the co-leaders of the firm's AFA initiative: Kathrine Cain, the manager of business intelligence, and Keri Gavin, the controller. Cain reported to the firm's director of business development, and Gavin reported to the firm's CFO, but they worked closely together to analyze the information that the firm needed for competitive pricing.

"The partners are encouraged to reach out to us for assistance with requests for alternative fee arrangements and budgets," Cain said.

> Some partners were already very good at defining budgets and pricing strategies, while some were new to the concepts. We coach them through the process of defining a budget and identifying pricing options that align with their client's needs and expectations. In the two years since starting the formal initiative, we have made significant strides in providing the tools and techniques to support our lawyers and clients.

Cain said she and Gavin always consider a wide range of options for AFA proposals, based on the client's expectations and goals as well as the projected internal rate of return, the anticipated level of staffing for the matter, benchmarks based on previous matters, the firm's history with that particular client, and other factors.

Fish & Richardson uses a somewhat different model. There, the AFA group is led by Kurt Glitzenstein, a firm partner and patent litigator.

Glitzenstein says that since his firm specializes in intellectual property law, many of his firm's cases fall into just a few categories, such as patent litigation. Fish & Richardson is able to ask the same questions in nearly every case and obtain useful answers that will help in its pricing.

"We prefer to price on an AFA basis," he said.

> To do that, my staff goes through a case and interviews the lead attorney about the details. Is it a judge whom we know well? How many patents are under litigation? What is the technology? How complex is it? As a result of inquiries like this, we can put together a litigation budget and use it as a guide for pricing. By asking the right questions, we can predict which cases will be more challenging to handle.
>
> We think that the fixed fee arrangements that Fish & Richardson often proposes improve aspects of the lawyer-client relationship. Fixed fees allow lawyers and clients to focus on the merits of the case so that they can reach the best result, without the same level of concern as in a traditional hourly fee arrangement, that changes to the case strategy, or unexpected developments, will significantly increase the cost to the client.

Of course, in every firm, ultimately the success or failure of this new pricing movement will depend on buy-in from the partners.

Mayer Brown's Byrd said that although it is not required that partners consult him when they need to respond to an RFP or develop an AFA proposal, it is highly recommended, and that his plate has been full.

Matt Laws, then head of the pricing program at Reed Smith, where just about 20% of the annual revenue comes from AFAs, said his role "Has been very well received… Partners do tend to call every time a potential engagement comes up."

Laws said Reed Smith does not have "any strict guidelines about what we can or cannot do to win a client's business. Any proactive approach to meeting a client's needs is likely to be approved."

In fact, Laws said, he sometimes finds himself and his team having direct contact with the clients' financial officers during the bidding process—something that would have been unthinkable only a few years ago. "In the old relationship, partners would work with corporate general counsel. Now, we see finance people and CFOs from the client companies. The process of online bidding, which has become more and more common, reduces the importance of the historical relationship between the firm and the client."

Another interesting trend in this area is a growing emphasis on project management. According to Baker & McKenzie's Dodds, "Over the last 18 months, the biggest change in the legal pricing field is a greater emphasis on project management and how we deliver services. Law firm clients are now looking for demonstrable value and efficiency, and we should not shy away from this challenge."

This should not be surprising, given that once a firm is committed to a fixed price or an hourly fee cap, the most important determinant of profitability is being able to meet the client's needs within a predetermined budget.

Firms are responding to these changes in a wide variety of ways, depending both on the firm's culture and available talent. Practice management staff are often involved in planning how to price proposals. To cite just one example, Womble Carlyle has identified Bill Turner, the director of practice management, as an internal point person to evaluate every significant price proposal in the firm and to analyze the pricing on every large RFP response.

The trend of appointing specialized pricing officials and devoting more effort to analyzing pricing is expected to increase. In 2011, ILTA, the International Legal Technology Association, formed a Financial Management Peer Group to develop a knowledge base of legal pricing resources and best practices. In the first full year of this peer group, membership grew from 12 people to over 140. According to steering committee member Toby Brown of Akin Gump, "As the group evolved it expanded its purpose to cover those working in legal project management, since many pricing positions were taking over or working directly on that set of tasks."

Using metrics to define value

In the legal profession, everybody's talking about value, but nobody seems to know how to measure it.

In September 2009, the Association of Corporate Counsel announced the creation of the ACC Value Index, a "client satisfaction measurement tool that helps ACC members to share meaningful information about the law firms they engage."[137] Clients were asked to rate law firms, using a scale of one to five, on six key factors:

- Understands objectives/expectations
- Efficiency/process management
- Predictable cost/budgeting skills
- Legal expertise
- Responsiveness/communication

- Results delivered/execution

Then they answered a single summary question: "Would you use this firm again?"

The idea of Zagat-type ratings of law firms was controversial from the start. In November 2011, ACC announced that the Value Index had been closed because "ACC members voted 'with their feet' by continuing to use the eGroups for law firm referrals, instead of the Value Index."[138]

While the idea of a Zagats of law firms has disappeared for now, the six key factors in its rating system remain a great starting point for defining value. The key phrase in that sentence is "starting point."

In a panel discussion at a 2011 Georgetown Law School Symposium entitled "Value: How do we define it? How do we measure it?" Susan Hackett, then head of the ACC Value Challenge, noted that "Value is hard to define.... The ACC Value Index offered an early set of categories of common interest to examine but it needs to move to the next level of assessment. The future of value assessment will be data-driven."[139]

Thought leaders are beginning to discuss exactly what value metrics should look like and how they should be related to prices. Paul Lippe has listed several value metrics that might be used to evaluate sales contracts:

- How quickly did the contract get done?
- How favorable are the terms to the company (opportunity gained and risk avoided)?
- How easy are the terms for other parts of the company (finance, manufacturing, sales, etc.) to understand and perform?
- How satisfied were the true business clients?

- How satisfied was the counterparty?
- How much did the contract cost?
- Did the contracting process improve?[140]

If you want to explore just how complicated this type of measurement can get in the real world, see the series entitled "A Value-based Client-firm Relationship" on the ACC's web page.[141] It includes 16 posts in which a client—Ken Grady, general counsel and secretary at Wolverine Worldwide—and his law firm—Seyfarth Shaw, represented by Lisa Damon—talk through the details of how they defined value metrics and determined cost for work on a trademark portfolio.

Here is one list of possible value metrics from the law firm side early in their negotiation:

- "Success" rate, measured by things like first action allowance, watch hit outcome
- Overall satisfaction
- Timeliness of communication
- Effectiveness of "lessons learned" sessions
- Strategic participation/understanding of Wolverine business
- Proactive issue identification
- Budget variance
- Cost management effectiveness[142]

Here are a few of the value metrics that the client proposed:

- Trademark Risk Rate (total dollars spent defending trademarks, divided by total number of trademarks defended)

- Counterfeit Recovery Rate (total dollars spent on anti-counterfeiting actions, divided by total number of units seized)
- Specimen Response Productivity (days from first request for specimen to receipt of acceptable specimen, divided by number of trademarks for which specimens requested).[143]

On the positive side, if you read all 16 posts about the details of this relationship, it is clear that the two sides developed a very trusting relationship, and that Seyfarth went the extra mile to be a proactive strategic partner that puts its money where its mouth is. On the negative side, this is uncharted territory, and it took months of discussion to come up with metrics that enabled both sides to measure how the process was going.

When the time came to tie the metrics to a portfolio price for the year, Grady proposed, "One way to set the new fee relationship for year one of the relationship would be to:

- Adjust the baseline based on what we know about the business (that is, increase, decrease or the same amount of portfolio activity)
- Adjust that amount to account for improvements in the processes to handle the portfolio using lean activities we will undertake with Seyfarth
- Adjust that amount to build in whatever cost-sharing is appropriate for Seyfarth to get up to speed on our business as reflected in the portfolio
- We then could agree on a base price to handle the portfolio work. We can gainshare on additional improvements—we get part of the benefit (lower costs) and Seyfarth gets part of the benefit (we don't get 100% of the lower costs). We could add a topper fee: depending on performance against certain other metrics

> (e.g., increase in average mark value using the equation I showed in the last post), Seyfarth gets an additional payment for helping to drive the increased average mark value."[144]

Here is one small part of how the payment system actually worked:

> To measure Seyfarth's systemic improvements, we will use two metrics: time to process an application, and time to receive a useable specimen (we have to file specimens in certain countries to show we are still using the mark). We need one score across both metrics to determine Seyfarth's bonus, so we will combine the results on the two metrics by weighting them 80% on trademark applications and 20% on specimen gathering. We calculate the trademark application improvement metric, multiply it by 0.8, calculate the process improvement on specimens metric, multiply it by 0.2, and add the results. For every X% of weighted process improvement, Seyfarth will earn $0.75.[145]

This example is much more sophisticated, complicated and demanding than the simple value pricing example quoted above from Baker's book, in which a client simply paid a hefty premium because he felt that he had received value in excess of hourly rates.[146]

There can be little doubt that in the current environment, some clients will continue to look for metrics that allow them to precisely define value and tie it to payment. But we predict that many lawyers will see the example above as excessively complicated, with a whole lot of arithmetic and price uncertainty. So it is far less certain how many clients and law firms will ultimately develop and use metrics like this.

Statistical variation in metrics

For those who want to tie metrics to payment, it is important to be aware of some basic statistical concepts that could affect how much you are paid.

Many of the metrics discussed above are averages. In court cases where data averages are at issue, statistical experts sometimes testify about the implications of confidence intervals.

Consider the example of estimating hours worked for a simple legal task for a particular client based on historical records. Suppose you find that the task was performed five times last year, and that the hours billed for these five instances were 51, 58, 43, 56 and 42.

The average of those five numbers is 50, so you estimate that this is a 50-hour task. Such an estimate with a single number is called a point estimate. However, statisticians would be quick to remind you that this estimate is only for a particular sample of five copies of the task. Even if all other things are equal, five similar matters next year might not come out with the same average.

To reflect the possible variability of the average hours needed for the task, you need to have a plausible range for the actual average—a confidence interval for the hours needed for the task. If you were to calculate the confidence interval for this data, you would find that there is a 95% probability that your average would fall between 41 and 59. Note that this implies there is also a 5% chance your average would be less than 41 or more than 59. The confidence interval is so large because you based your conclusion on only five point estimates. If your average had been based on 50 or 500 points, the law of large numbers would lead to a much narrower confidence interval.

This may seem surprising if you never took statistics, or long ago forgot the difference between chi squared and sigma. But it may be important in pricing. If you base a fixed fee on 50 hours of work, your average next year for this task may turn out to be much lower or much higher. Sometimes you will win, and sometimes you will lose. The smaller your initial sample, the greater the variability and risk.

You don't need a Ph.D. in math to estimate confidence intervals, you just need someone who knows how to use the statistical functions built into Excel. And even more important than the specific numbers is a general awareness that no matter how good a lawyer you are, point estimates are an imperfect predictor of the future.

Where firms are today

As we noted in Chapter 6, when law firms begin offering non-hourly AFAs, they must address two fundamental questions:

1. When bidding for new work, how do I set a price that is high enough to protect profits, but low enough to get the work?
2. After winning the work, how do I manage the matter so that I make a profit (or at least break even) at that price?

To be honest, when I started writing about legal pricing, I thought that my research would be limited to the first question: picking a price in the first place. This requires external knowledge about your client and the marketplace, and internal knowledge about your own cost structure.

But the more I talked to people and reviewed the literature, the more obvious it became that the two questions are so wrapped up in each other that they are very hard to separate. That's one of the reasons I ended up writing this single book about all three topics: pricing, AFAs, and project management.

Add in the fact that many lawyers don't even understand their own costs of doing business and that price wars are forcing bids down for many practice areas, and you have the makings of a very complex situation.

Many lawyers would like to believe that if they could master the art of value pricing, they could make more money than ever before. Maybe some can. But with competition constantly forcing prices lower, I have not seen much evidence for that yet. Some believe that pricing will become more sensible when lawyers learn how to develop value metrics, but I remain to be convinced.

The two questions above are so difficult that firms like Baker & McKenzie, Akin Gump, Mayer Brown and others are setting up pricing directors and committees to help answer them, case by case.

In many firms, influential partners have great latitude or even complete control over pricing, so they must understand the principles before they will accept help from a pricing director or committee. Some firms are moving to develop policies which limit partners' power to set prices depending on their training and experience, but these policies are very much a work in progress.

No matter how a firm is organized, pricing analyses inevitably get pulled into the question of how to manage matters. To set the right price, you must know what the work requires. In the good old days when lawyers did not have to worry about how much things cost, that was relatively straightforward. But now that so many clients are demanding efficiency, the work must be done differently. That will inevitably change the cost of delivering a quality service, and ultimately its price.

Which takes the pricing discussion full circle back to LPM.

If we needed to summarize where legal pricing stands today in a single phrase, it would be "in transition."

Predicting the future of pricing

What do the changes in efficiency imply for the next 10 years, or the next 10 months? Nobody knows.

In a blog post entitled "Staying Relevant," Toby Brown recently put it this way:

> We have reached a point in human history where predicting the future beyond a few years is quite a challenge. A perfect example is that of Facebook, which grew from zero to 100 million users in less than two years. What things will look like in five to ten years is anyone's guess. So the best we can do now is keep a vigilant eye on the storm and stay prepared to constantly alter course.[147]

While we don't know exactly how things will turn out, it does seem safe to predict that changes in pricing will be driven by eight key trends:

1. **Alternative fee arrangements will continue to increase.** As explained in Chapter 8, at least 15% of legal fees are currently non-hourly, and the percentage is growing. Conservative clients often require a long time to take the leap to try non-hourly fees, but this particular change is a one-way street. Once they succeed with AFAs, they will not go back.
2. **Lawyers will develop new metrics that measure value.** Sophisticated clients want to measure what they are paying for, and a sophisticated law firm should be able to measure its own results. Above we gave an extended example of the challenge of one past attempt to define value metrics. For an interesting discussion of why there is resistance to this idea, see Paul Lippe's blog post entitled, "What If Someone Could Measure What Lawyers Do?" and the comments written by various lawyers at the end of that piece.[148]

3. **Leading firms and clients will place increasing emphasis on aligning their interests.** One key to success for AFAs is creating a genuine sense of partnership by aligning interests. As one AmLaw 100 decision maker put it in our *LegalBizDev Survey of Alternate Fees*:

   > The firm and the client must have a very transparent conversation about the process. [It is important to discuss] how [the fee structure] will be mapped out and who will do what. [It is vital] to look at the delivery of services holistically, and to look at how the team in-house and the team outside can work together to deliver value for your shared client. That's a real challenge, because it is tricky to transition from a negotiation process to a collaborative process. If you can get into a collaborative discussion, you can get good results that work for both organizations.[149]

   This requires some sharing of risk. Another participant in our survey said, "GCs should be thinking about what kind of risks they are willing to take early on in the life of a particular matter. Right now, they want firms to take all the risk and they are reluctant to take risks themselves."[150]

4. **The distinction between bet the company, important and commodity work will be reflected in different pricing strategies.** In Chapter 6, we quoted Jim Durham's 2005 estimates that about 5% of legal work fell into the "bet the company" category, 65-70% was "important" and 25-30% commodity work. There is every indication that since then the percentage of commodity work has gone up, and the other two categories have shrunk. To be price competitive, it will be crucial to keep up with the process improvement and outsourcing alternatives for commodity work. As Brown noted in his blog series "Staying Relevant:"

An emerging and compelling reason for lawyers to make different business decisions is coming from new breeds of competitors. One example is the Legal Process Outsourcer (LPO) market. These companies started as off-shore (typically India) based providers for first document review in litigation. They hire English speaking, American law trained candidates in other, lower wage countries. These much lower-costing, well-enough trained lawyers were appropriately suited for this level of work. So well-matched to the tasks, that in very short order, these document reviewers became viable competitors. Most lawyers glossed over this market encroachment, seeing it as commodity level work no longer worthy of their skills. In reality, this meant millions in fees were no longer going to US lawyers.[151]

5. **Law firm profitability will be squeezed harder than ever before**. According to the *2012 Client Advisory* from the Hildebrandt Institute and Citi Private Bank, "many firms will need to work harder to maintain profitability at levels that meet the expectations of their partners."[152]

6. **Hourly billing and high partner profits will be questioned more and more in the future.** Clients generally do not live in an hourly billing world. They know their actual costs of doing business and plan to make a profit above those costs. They have pricing risks and plans to manage those risks. Clients often wonder why their law firms cannot do the same. Many corporate counsel started their careers as associates at large firms, and they know all too well how the profit model works for firms. Many are asking why partner compensation is so high. As Susan Hackett put it:

    Surveys—such as these from Corporate Counsel and Empsight—are coming out. They usually confirm that the average in-house counsel who hires outside firms makes only slightly north of what a bonused first- or second-year associate in a big law firm makes. There are a few hundred large law department top leaders who haul in comparable returns for their work—usually through non-salary comp—but nowhere near the number or percentage of highly compensated partners that we find in the ranks at big firms where entire equity partnerships pull in hundreds of thousands or over $1 million a year in profit per partner.

The average in-house lawyer is well aware that he shares with those high-profiting partners the same schooling, sophisticated law firm background, and top-flight experience on his resume. He's made his choice, but please remember that he will more likely identify with the "99 percent"—and not the partnership—when he's assessing who's getting coal this Christmas.[153]

7. **Competition on price and value will increase.** The Hildebrandt/CitiBank *2012 Client Advisory* also notes that, "[There is] continuing client resistance to fee increases [and]… it is unlikely… that the demand for legal services will grow robustly for the foreseeable future…. The legal industry will be forced to live with uncertainty for some time to come."[154] With some law firms aggressively providing more value at lower prices, the competitive bar is going up.

Whatever else may prove to be true, it seems clear that cost will remain a major issue. As Mark Smith put it in a blog post entitled, "Excuse me, I think your pricing is broken:"

> The common refrain from private practice lawyers… is that in-house lawyers who talk about value based billing really just want to pay less, and are not really interested in concepts like sharing risk. Opening a dialogue about pricing is simply an exercise in

getting the law firm to do the same work for less money.

Of course they want to pay less!

The fact that the firm hasn't developed a model that really meets their needs… does not turn this into the client's problem. It's the private practice lawyer's problem. It's the firm's problem. It's the profession's problem.

The market has changed.

Forever.[155]

8. **Law firms will continue to put more emphasis on pricing and project management.** When I conducted the *LegalBizDev Survey of Alternative Fees* in 2009, I thought the most insightful quote in the entire research dealt with pricing. It came from a senior partner who had previously worked in-house:

> For most of the past decade, I was a senior executive at a publicly-traded real estate company, and I like to say that the two most important people we had in the company were the estimator and the project manager. Law firms historically have had no one play either of those roles. It's very dangerous to move into a world of fixed fees if you don't have somebody who's capable of estimating and you don't have somebody who's capable of project managing it.

In the years since that survey was conducted, law firms have begun working to fill both those roles, sometimes with individuals, sometimes with departments, and sometimes with entirely new ways of doing business. All signs point to an ever-faster pace of change.

Chapter 8
Alternatives to the billable hour

In 2002, the American Bar Association published its influential *ABA Commission on Billable Hours Report.*[156] The report summarized the conclusions of a distinguished panel of experts who had studied the pros and cons of billing by the hour.

The commission found that "the overreliance on billable hours by the legal profession:

- Results in a decline of the collegiality of law firm culture and an increase in associate departures
- Discourages taking on pro bono work
- Does not encourage project or case planning
- Provides no predictability of cost for client
- May not reflect value to the client
- Penalizes the efficient and productive lawyer
- Discourages communication between lawyer and client
- Encourages skipping steps

- Fails to discourage excessive lawyering and duplication of effort
- Fails to promote a risk/benefit analysis
- Does not reward the lawyer for productive use of technology
- Puts client's interests in conflict with lawyer's interests
- The client runs the risk of paying for:
  - The lawyer's incompetency or inefficiency
  - Associate training
  - Associate turnover
  - Padding of timesheets
- Results in itemized bills that tend to report mechanical functions, not value of progress
- Results in lawyers competing based on hourly rates"[157]

Later in the report, the Commission highlighted the most critical problem:

> Hourly billing allows, indeed may encourage, profligate work habits. A *cost-plus* contract can degenerate into disregard for basic market discipline. So too can the obvious benefit of being paid for working more hours lead, directly or indirectly, to inflating the number of hours worked. Cost-plus can also override scruples about quarter-hour billing increments, which are never marked down, only up.[158]

If the billable hour has all these inherent problems, why does it continue to dominate the legal profession? As David Sump of Troutman & Sanders wrote in the *Newsletter of the Virginia Bar Association* a few years ago, "The billable hour dies hard, like a cockroach that refuses to check into its own special motel or a rodent that scoffs at the spring-loaded cheese morsel... I must confess that as much as I detest the billable hour, I know that if we bill enough of them each month, there will be money left over at the end of the month to pay my partners."[159]

In part, the billable hour continues to dominate the legal world because it is simple and straightforward, and everyone is comfortable with it. But also, in the words of the ABA commission, because it "Lets law firms make more money."[160]

The seductive appeal of hourly billing is a problem in every profession, not just in legal circles. In my experience owning and operating a training and consulting company for more than 25 years, I've found that hourly contracts are habit-forming. Before we started working with lawyers, one of our biggest clients was the US Government, and almost all of our $15 million in government contracts were on an hourly basis.

From the government's point of view, the job we did was good enough to win several awards.[161] But from our point of view, the business model of billing by the hour created a disturbing conflict of interest.

The only way to make more money was to hire more people. The more efficient we became, the less money we made. Our needs were fundamentally opposed to our clients' needs. It was bad for business relationships, bad for work habits, and bad for employee morale.

Nevertheless, we became addicted to hourly billing. Every time we had some success, we hired more people. That increased the number of hours we needed to bill the next month to break even.

When signing new business with non-government clients, we sometimes had a choice between a fixed price contract and an hourly approach. In those days, I always chose hourly, because I hate risk and the hourly approach minimized my risk.

A few years after our government contracts peaked, we switched our focus to helping lawyers develop new business, and renamed the company LegalBizDev. Since then, all of our work has been fixed price. The reason is ironic: Lawyers love to bill by the hour, but they hate to pay that way.

When I asked LegalBizDev Principal Steve Barrett about his 20 years of experience working for AmLaw 100 firms, he told me that he could remember only a few isolated instances in which they purchased services on an hourly basis. They know better.

The 2002 ABA report generated a great deal of discussion, but for several years it seemed to have little impact on behavior. A small percentage of clients and firms continued to use non-hourly AFA billing (as they had for many years before the report), but most ignored it.

Ron Baker, whose approach to value billing was described in Chapter 6, wrote a few years ago that a widespread switch away from hourly billing "Could take decades if not centuries, since it involves the diffusion of a theory. I was naive enough to think the ABA Report in 2002 would have an impact, but alas, it fell flat. I'm starting to think physicist Max Planck was right: progress happens funeral by funeral."[162]

But in 2008, two things happened that led to a new spurt of interest in AFAs: the economy declined, and the Association of Corporate Counsel announced its Value Challenge which held that "Many traditional law firm business models... are not aligned with what corporate clients want and need: value-driven, high-quality legal services that deliver solutions for a reasonable cost." These events have led to a gradual increase in the use of AFAs, along with some controversy about exactly how to define them (see Chapter 9), and even what to call them.

Some experts prefer the phrase "value fees" to refer to non-hourly arrangements. When the Association of Corporate

Counsel published a free guide to AFAs, they named it the *ACC Value-Based Fee Primer*. When Patrick Lamb wrote one of the best books on the topic, he used both terms in the title: *Alternative Fee Arrangements: Value Fees and the Changing Legal Market.*

In this book, I have avoided using the term value fees for two reasons. First, it can lead to the erroneous assumption that non-hourly fees must be based on the value pricing model described in Chapter 6. Some versions of value pricing can also lead to odd situations, as suggested by an anecdote in Lamb's book about a conversation with the head of one law firm who "Once told me of charging two clients two different amounts for what was essentially the same work because the work had different value to each client."[163]

Second, I think the phrase "value fees" puts too much emphasis on the client side of the table. What buyers want to pay is extremely important to price setting. But the cost to sellers matters, too—it takes two to tango.

AFA surveys

In 2009, when the AFA buzz was first building, we interviewed senior decision makers at 37 AmLaw 100 firms for the *LegalBizDev Survey of Alternative Fees*. Participants were recruited by contacting the chair or managing partner of every AmLaw 100 firm. Thirty-one interviews were conducted with a single individual, and six included two or three people at the same time. All told, we talked to nine chairmen and managing partners, 16 executives (including CEOs, CFOs and CMOs) and 22 senior partners, many of whom headed their firm's alternative fee committee.

The final report included hundreds of quotes about what works for AFAs, and what does not. The precise wording of every quote we published was approved in advance by the interviewee, but every statement was also anonymous. This confidential approach encouraged senior decision makers to speak frankly and openly, and provided a platform that made it easy for firm leaders to say what they really thought, without being quoted by name. Here's what one of them said about the transition from hourly billing to AFAs: "When it comes to alternative billing arrangements, a number of clients are just not sure yet what it is they are looking for. They are feeling their way through this paradigm shift, just as we are."

In the words of another senior partner in our survey, the whole discussion was also "like a junior high dance. There's a lot more talking than dancing."

While that comment still rings true today, surveys have consistently found that the use of AFAs is slowly growing. In Altman Weil's *2012 Law Firms in Transition Survey*, 47% of firms reported that their AFA revenue had increased in the past year. In the *2012 ALM Legal Intelligence Survey*, 50% of law departments and 62% of law firms reported that there was an increase in the volume of AFAs in the preceding year. And in the American Lawyer's *2012 Law Firm Leaders Survey*, 68% said more clients are requesting AFAs.[164]

While it is crystal clear that the use of AFAs is growing, it is impossible to be sure exactly what percent of law firm revenue they currently represent. There are many reasons this question is difficult to answer, including disagreements over the definition of the term "alternative fee arrangements," law firm secrecy about finances, and the fact that many firms simply do not know.

When I conducted the *LegalBizDev Survey of Alternative Fees* in 2009, one of the questions I asked AmLaw 100 decision makers was, "Does your accounting system code alternative fee projects separately, so that you can easily look up the exact percent of last year's revenue from alternative fees at your firm?" At that time, only about one in four could look up AFA revenue. (66% answered no, and another 7% did not know.) When I asked decision makers in that same survey to estimate the average revenue percentage for the AmLaw 100 as a whole, answers were all over the map, ranging from 1% of revenue to 25%.

While the answers would be a bit more precise if that survey were repeated today, there is still no definitive revenue data, and firms are far short of 100% certainty.

When ALM's Law Firm Leaders survey asked firms to report their average percent of AFA revenue in 2010, the figure was 16%. Unfortunately, as of the date this book was written, no systematic studies of law firms have repeated this question since 2010. In its *2011 Chief Legal Officer survey* (but not in the 2012 version), Altman Weil asked the same question of in-house legal departments and came up with a figure of 14%.

Given all this, including the fact that none of the samples in any of these studies were random, an academic-oriented researcher might say that the answer to the AFA revenue question is "no one really knows." However, most consultants would probably accept the conclusion that the percentage of law firm revenue derived from non-hourly AFAs is currently over 15% and growing. While in some ways 15% may not sound like much, it is important to emphasize that this implies that the AmLaw 100 alone performed over $10 billion worth of legal work last year on a non-hourly basis (based on 15% times their total gross revenue of about $71 billion).

When ALM Legal Intelligence surveyed 141 law departments and 194 large law firms about AFAs, they asked both to rate the major benefits.[165] For law departments—the buyers—the top three answers were cost predictability/transparency (87%), cost savings (68%) and increased efficiency—e.g. quality and value for legal service (44%). When they asked law firms—the sellers—the same question, the top three benefits were quite different: attracting or maintaining clients (91%), simplified billing and operations (50%) and increased billing realization (43%).

The first benefit—attracting and maintaining clients—was named by more than nine out of 10 firms, and far outdistanced the others. Based on off-the-record discussions, I think some lawyers would phrase this motivation another way: "We are offering AFAs because we have to." The use of AFAs in marketing is discussed in Chapter 11.

AFA profitability

The *ABA Commission on Billable Hours Report* predicted that the non-hourly approach would be a financial boon to law firms: "Alternatives that encourage efficiency and improve processes… increase profits"[166]

Some consultants love to spread this good news message, and when law firms and law departments talk publicly about the topic, they too often focus on the upbeat side. For example, in an article entitled "Alternative Fees for Litigation: Improved Control and Higher Value," James D. Shomper and Gardner G. Courson argue that "if properly structured, an alternative fee arrangement should result in a win-win scenario for client and law firm."[167]

To cite just one more example, a New York Times article about alternative fees quoted Carl A. Leonard, a former chairman of Morrison & Foerster, about AFA profit potential:

> In one case... Morrison & Foerster negotiated a fixed fee for defending a company in court, covering work up to the point of a motion for summary judgment.

> On top of the fee, if the case settled for less than what the company feared having to pay if it lost in court, the law firm got a percentage of the amount saved. The arrangement made sense when the goal was to resolve the dispute quickly....
>
> Lawyers on the case negotiated a settlement for much less than the client's worst-case number, Mr. Leonard said. "The effective hourly rate was something like 150 percent of our hourly rates," he added. "We made money, the client was happy."[168]

I think such examples are the exception to the rule and believe it can be very hard to turn fixed prices into win-wins, especially in a highly competitive market. My view has been shaped by my personal experience running my fixed price and hourly projects in my own business. For more than 25 years, I have found that consistently profiting from fixed fee work is an enormous challenge, and a struggle that never ends.

In the hundreds of fixed fee projects we've performed, the vast majority were a zero-sum game. In the short run, when the project was over, one party did better than they would have on an hourly basis, and the other party did worse. Usually the client had power over the deal terms, and we were the one that did worse.

Fixed price projects begin with planning a budget upfront and then managing the work to keep within that budget as the project proceeds. When my company was billing by the hour, I found it relatively easy to maximize billing and profitability. If an employee had nothing to do on one project, I could usually find something for them to do on another, and keep them billing.

But during periods with a significant amount of fixed price work, it became extremely difficult to juggle dozens of projects with ever-changing deadlines in such a way that everyone remained billable and projects stayed within budget. And during mixed periods, when some of our projects were fixed price and some were billed hourly, it was an absolute nightmare. Employees quickly understood the never-spoken message that while they needed to be efficient on fixed price projects, inefficiency was winked at or even encouraged in hourly projects. For some employees, this inconsistent message created a conflict that threatened to make their heads explode.

Lawyers have been rewarded for their entire careers for putting in extra hours to analyze every risk from every possible angle. Many will have a hard time learning to deliver the quality they are comfortable with when they must work within strict funding limits. And law firm managers will have an even greater challenge when they try to juggle staff on dozens or hundreds of projects with constantly shifting deadlines. Traditionally, most firms expect lawyers to bill 1,800 hours per year or more. If firms shift a significant portion of their work to a fixed price basis, many will find that goal unreachable.

When both inside and outside counsel talk about alternative fee arrangements, I predict they will continue to accentuate the positive, and focus on win-wins. People will speak most freely about the matters that make them feel good and look good. But in my experience as a business owner, in fixed price deals one side usually wins a revenue concession and the other side does less well.

When I wrote about this a few years ago in my blog, Jordan Furlong, now a consultant at Edge International, made this incisive comment:

> It may come down to how we define "winning." I think a win-win alternative-billing scenario right now might look like this: the client wins because it reduces its outside legal spend, or at least improves its legal cost certainty, and the law firm wins because it gets to keep

> the client for one more day. That's not the kind of victory lawyers are accustomed to settling for, but I think they ought to get used to it.[169]

One of the biggest pressures on AFA profitability is the fact that in many firms, lawyers are paid more if they bill more hours. Several participants in the *LegalBizDev Survey of Alternative Fees* noted that without proper management, AFAs can be seen as a giant loophole, a place where lawyers who have too little to do can bill as many hours as they like, without risking client complaints:

> It takes a lot of discipline to manage a contingent matter. When lawyers track hours on a traditional hourly project, they know that clients will review the results, and that creates a certain discipline. On contingent matters, lawyers may think no one will look at the hourly record for years.
>
> One of the lessons [we've] learned is that somebody has to be the point for cost control. It often happens that alternative fee matters, particularly large ones, [end up being] a dumping ground for individuals who may not be fully employed because you are reportable to the client for the result, not the cost. [When lawyers work unnecessarily on a project] your profitability looks bad, so in order to really determine the profitability, we need to deal with that issue.

Some relationship partners we've worked with encourage associates to put in extra hours on AFA matters. Associate salaries are a sunk cost, the partners reason, so they might as well put in extra time to assure quality and client satisfaction on fixed fee matters. It's more productive than googling or staring out the window.

In the short term, they have a point. But in the long term, this type of thinking is highly counter-productive. It reinforces the bad habits created by decades of hourly billing, and substantially increases the chances that AFAs will be unprofitable.

It is not surprising that systematic data on AFA profitability is hard to come by. Law firms are notoriously secretive about their finances, sometimes even with their own partners. And nobody likes to publicize their losses.

In Chapter 6, we talked about competitive pressures to cut prices. We also talked about the results of the best available data on the topic of AFA profitability. When Altman Weil's *2012 Law Firms in Transition Survey* asked "compared to projects billed at an hourly rate, are your firm's non-hourly projects more profitable or less profitable?" the results were 14% more profitable, 40% the same, 29% less profitable, and 17% not sure.

Even more interesting were Altman Weil's findings about which firms profited.

Some law firms have for years proactively used AFAs as a way to increase new business, and invested in training and systems to make them more profitable. For example, at Morgan Lewis, says Richard Rosenblatt, the operations partner for the Labor and Employment Practice, "AFAs invite the client to engage with us and increase the ties that bind. We're now on the same team, and more likely to get the next engagement. This is an opportunity to get a bigger share of a shrinking pie."

When Altman Weil asked, "Is your firm's use of alternative fee arrangements primarily reactive (in response to client requests) or primarily proactive (arising from your belief in the competitive advantage of alternative fees)?" about one-third said they were proactive (33.2%) and two-thirds classified themselves as reactive.

When Altman Weil compared AFA profitability for the two groups, they found that it pays to be proactive: "Firms that are proactive rather than reactive in their use of AFAs are more than three times as likely to enjoy higher profitability on their non-hourly work."[170] We will have more to say about this proactive approach in Chapter 11.

Predicting the future of AFAs

Where are we headed? Almost everyone agrees that the legal profession is changing, but there are significant differences of opinion about how much it will change and how soon.

Lawyers who would like to believe that non-hourly arrangements will go the way of pet rocks and Boy George often quote client reluctance as a reason to believe that AFAs are just a passing fad. In our *LegalBizDev Survey of Alternative Fees*, many AmLaw 100 decision makers commented on clients' initial reluctance to make the switch:

> At least half of the time, maybe more, when the client says alternative fee, what they are really saying is, "Give me a larger [hourly] discount than you gave me before."
>
> What we hear regularly, probably every week, is, "Wow, that was such an innovative fee proposal. It was really good to see that your firm is thinking outside the box and is willing to take risks and partner up with us, and put skin in the game. Now let's talk about how much of a discount you'll give us."[171]

But it is important to distinguish between the difficulty of taking the first step away from hourly, and the ease of continuing down that path. This particular change is a one-way street, and there is no turning back.

In 2010, Tucker Ellis became one of the first firms with over 100 lawyers to generate more than half their revenue from non-hourly work. When I interviewed their managing partner Joe Morford about this trend for my blog, he noted that many clients were initially reluctant to make the switch, but that, "Once we started working for a client with alternative fees, not a single one has wanted to go back."

Clients saw for themselves that, as Morford put it, "If you pay for hours you get hours, and if you pay for results you get results."[172]

If you are skeptical about this trend, consider the situation from a client's point of view. If you hire someone to redesign your kitchen or fix your car, would you prefer to pay by the hour or to get a fixed price you know you could count on?

Surveys report a consistent belief that AFAs will continue to grow. In the *2012 ALM Legal Intelligence Survey*, 76% of law departments and 74% of law firms predicted that AFAs will increase in the next five years. And in Altman Weil's *2012 Law Firms in Transition Survey*, 80% said they think that "more non-hourly billing will be a permanent trend going forward."

Of course, it is impossible to predict just how quickly this move to alternative fees will proceed, or when it will reach a tipping point.

As explained in Chapter 4, of all the firms that have moved in the direction of greater efficiency and non-hourly billing, none has generated more publicity than Seyfarth Shaw. In 2006, they started using Six Sigma and process improvement techniques to simplify and standardize legal work, and ultimately created a proprietary system called Seyfarth*Lean*. But if Seyfarth Shaw is at the head of this movement, it is interesting to note that six years into the effort, Seyfarth Chairman Steve Poor wrote in the New York Times DealBook: "Never underestimate the resistance to change from lawyers."

Chapter 9
Types of AFAs

When the Association of Corporate Counsel asked 1,165 chief legal officers about the types of AFAs they used most often, they found that 8% of all legal work was performed for a fixed fee, 2% for retainers, and 1% on a contingency basis.[173] The remaining 89% was hourly.[174]

Nine common types of AFAs

In the *LegalBizDev Survey of Alternative Fees*, we identified the nine types of fees that are most commonly used by AmLaw 100 firms.

Nine common types of AFAs	
Fee caps	In a fee cap, hourly rates are charged up to an agreed maximum amount for a particular matter. Beyond that, if additional work is required to complete the matter, the law firm pays for it. Of course, this is really just hourly billing with a twist: a hard limit on the maximum. Some lawyers see fee caps as the worst of both worlds—you can do worse than hourly, but you can't do better—and refuse to do business this way. While this arrangement does clearly benefit the client more than the law firm, other firms see fee caps as an inevitable element of the changing legal landscape, and an important way to get new work.
Fixed fees for single engagements	A fixed fee for a single engagement sets a firm price for a set of well-defined services. In order to succeed with this approach over the long run, firms must do many such deals, since they will surely win some and lose some. This arrangement can be risky with new clients, until mutual trust and understanding has been established.

Nine common types of AFAs	
Fixed fee menus	A fixed fee menu provides a list of fees for related services, or for segments of a particular matter. For example, a fee of $25,000 might be quoted for a particular type of real estate transaction. Then charges would be added to this base for different situations, such as $5,000 more for assumption of an existing loan, $5,000 for a joint equity partner, and $7,500 for new financing.
Portfolio fixed fees	Portfolio fixed fees set a single price for a large number of matters, such as all of a Fortune 100 company's US labor and employment cases in a single year. As in other fixed fee arrangements, the key to success is to have a large number of matters, so that there will be enough wins to offset the inevitable losses.
Retainers	A retainer is a fee that a client agrees to pay every month, or on some other regular basis, in return for specified services. These have been used for many years, and come in several forms, ranging from a deposit on hourly work to a true fixed price arrangement. Many firms see them as a great marketing tool, since clients are more likely to pick up the phone than they would be if they were paying by the hour, and this can lead to discussions of other new business.

Nine common types of AFAs	
Partial contingencies/ Success fees	In a partial contingency arrangement, a law firm typically receives part of its normal hourly fees as a matter proceeds, and a lump sum—or success fee—at the end of the matter, depending on the result. Criteria for success fees are sometimes spelled out at length, and sometimes left entirely to the client's discretion. Clearly this can have the benefit of aligning the interests of clients and their law firms.
Holdbacks	A holdback is a type of partial contingency arrangement in which the law firm is guaranteed part of its fees, but the other part is contingent upon the case's success. For example, a firm may receive 80% of its normal rates while a matter is underway. At the end, it may be given the remaining 20%, or less, depending on the client's satisfaction with the result. This may also be combined with a success fee that provides a bonus for a positive result.
Full contingencies	In a full contingency arrangement, fees depend entirely on success. This approach has long been used by plaintiffs' lawyers, but it is now becoming more common for the defense to use as well.

Nine common types of AFAs	
Risk collars	Lawyers use the term risk collar to refer to an hourly billing arrangement built around an estimated budget for a particular matter. The client pays a bonus if work is completed under budget and/or gets a discount if the work goes over the budget. Like a fee cap, this is really just a variation on hourly work, but unlike a fee cap it may align interests and offer incentives to both clients and law firms. The actual discounts and bonuses vary widely. The table below includes six examples of actual deals described by survey participants.

Examples of different types of risk collars		
	If work is completed under budget, firm gets:	If work goes over budget, firm offers:
Example 1	Normal hourly rates, no bonus	First 15% over budget for free, then "at a very reduced rate"
Example 2	Normal hourly rates, no bonus	25% discount on all hours over budget
Example 3	Normal hourly rates plus a bonus if they are more than 10% under budget	Discounted rate on hours more than 10% over budget
Example 4	50% of the savings on all hours under budget	50% discount on all hours over budget
Example 5	50% of the savings on all hours under budget	First 20% over for free, 75% discount on 21-40% over, 50% discount on 41% over or more
Example 6	75% of the savings on all hours under budget	25% refund for any hours over budget

Is our list of nine types the definitive typology of AFA variations? No. It's as good a choice as any other list, but there is no definitive typology. As Patrick Lamb of Valorem has put it, there are "a limitless variety of ways to structure fees."

For example, when ALM Legal Intelligence conducted their survey of AFAs,[175] they used a slightly different list and found the percent of firms who used each type of AFA as shown in this graph:

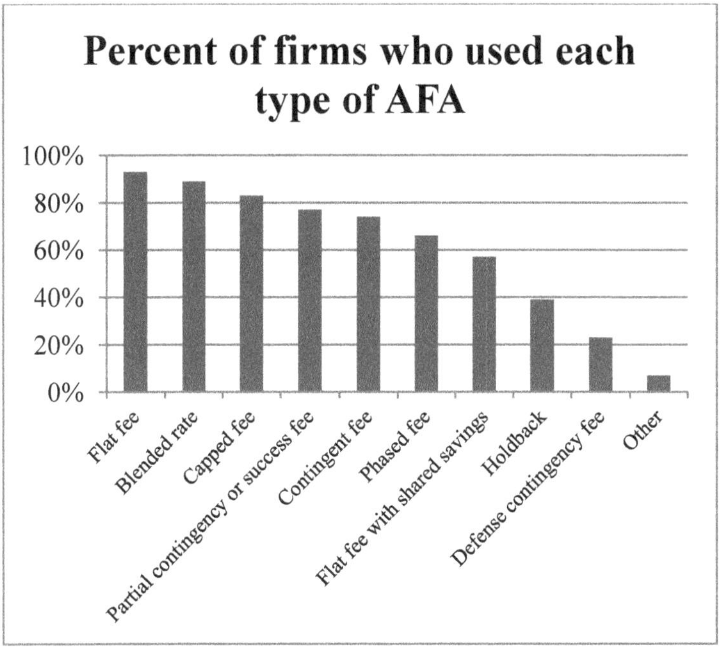

In general, these categories cover the same ground as our nine types, using different terminology and grouping them in a slightly different way.[176] However, there is one difference that is quite important: the *ALM Legal Intelligence Survey* classified blended rates as an AFA, and our survey specifically excluded them.

Are blended rates AFAs?

Blended rates are 100% hourly arrangements, in which a single middle rate is charged for senior lawyers who normally charge more and junior lawyers who normally charge less. Whether the client or the firm benefits from this arrangement depends on the actual numbers in a particular situation.

For example, consider a case that is expected to require 100 hours of senior time at an average of $500 per hour ($50,000) and 100 hours of junior time at $300 per hour ($30,000), for a total of $80,000. A firm might offer a blended rate of $350 per hour, which reduces the predicted cost of the matter to $70,000 ($350 times 200 hours).

But now suppose that once the matter is underway, the firm discovers that almost all the work could actually be performed by more junior lawyers. If the senior lawyers only need to spend 20 hours supervising the matter (which would have cost $10,000 at the original rate of $500 times 20 hours), and junior lawyers put in the other 180 hours (which would have cost $54,000 at $300 times 180 hours), the client who pays the blended rate will actually pay more ($70,000) at the blended rate than they would have at the non-discounted rate ($64,000).

Now you could argue that it's still a win-win, because if the firm had not offered blended rates, senior lawyers would have delivered 100 hours out of the 200. The client won by paying $70,000 instead of $80,000, and the firm won by charging $70,000 instead of $64,000.

From a marketing perspective, that is a terrible argument. In essence, it implies that senior people never should have been doing the work in the first place and the client must agree to be overcharged a little in order to avoid being overcharged a lot.

Blended rates invite gamesmanship, as individual lawyers may be tempted to manipulate predictions to maximize profit. And they encourage the use of more junior level lawyers, even when it may not be to the client's benefit. Here's how the general counsel at Marriott International described his unhappiness with his blended rate experience: "The law firm only assigned to the matter those lawyers whose regular hourly rate was at or below the blended rate, and more senior lawyers were unwilling to engage in significant supervision."[177]

We will leave it to others to argue about whether blended rates are a good thing or a bad thing. In this context, what is important is that there is a philosophical difference between two types of AFA definitions: narrow and broad. Our survey used the narrow definition which reserves the term AFAs for fees that are fully or partly non-hourly. The broad definition used by the ALM survey and others also includes blended rates which are 100% hourly, but offer a single hourly rate that applies to all lawyers on a matter.

People feel very strongly about which definition should be used. When members of our Advisory Board reviewed a draft of this book, some said that we made a mistake and that blended rates should be considered AFAs. Others said we made the opposite mistake and needed to be much more forceful in explaining that "blended rates ***are not*** alternative fee arrangements and are no different than discounting."

The fact that two conflicting definitions of AFAs are in wide use adds considerable confusion to an area that was already confusing enough. If a firm claims that 50% of its work is performed on an alternative fee basis, that could mean that they are moving away from the billable hour (under the narrow definition), or it could mean that they are engaging in some creative hourly rate discounting (under the broad definition).

Some have a vested interest in maintaining this confusion. Announcing that a firm offers 50% of its work on an alternative fee basis sounds much more thoughtful and less desperate than saying, "Half the time, we have to slash our hourly rates because we need the business."

About fixed fees

Fixed fees are the most common type of AFA, and account for 8% of all legal work according to ACC's Chief Legal Officer Survey.[178]

No one would argue that fixed fees are easy. Some professional project managers devote their entire working life to balancing quality and cost in fixed fee agreements.

But if you are just getting started with fixed fees, these eight steps will help you get started by drawing on best practices from other law firms and other professions:

Step 1. Identify the matters that are most suitable for a fixed fee

Repetitive and predictable cases are a good place to start because they are much easier to handle on a fixed price basis than one-of-a-kind cases.

Step 2. If necessary, break down large matters into smaller ones and into phases

If it is too hard to predict the requirements and price for a large matter that could extend over years, try setting a price for the next 90 days. Or consider whether a fixed price could be charged for phases, such as separate fixed fees for interrogatories, pretrial motions, and summary judgment motions.

Step 3. Actively discuss fixed price work with carefully selected clients

From a marketing perspective, the best reason to offer a fixed fee is because the client wants it.

Business development is all about advancing relationships with the right people. So it may be useful to raise the subject of fixed fees with each of your clients. At an absolute minimum, a discussion of alternative fees is a great excuse to spend time with clients understanding what they truly want and need.

However, there are also reasons for caution. Do not open the discussion if you are not in fact willing to offer a fixed price. You can't put the genie back in the bottle, and once you get a client thinking about fixed fees, it may be difficult to continue on an hourly basis.

If you are just starting to experiment with this approach, you may also want to start first with your B and C clients, to work the bugs out of the system. Approach your A clients only when you have a proven track record of success.

And if you lack a trusting relationship with a particular client, and think they may take advantage of a fixed price situation, proceed with caution or not at all.

Despite the benefits of predictability, some clients will not be interested in fixed fees. They may be risk-averse by nature, comfortable with hourly billing, and unwilling to take a chance on lawyers cutting corners to stay within budget. But most clients will still appreciate the offer to discuss fixed fees, if only because it shows that you are looking for better ways to meet their needs.

Step 4. Identify factors that drive cost up, and consider how you might control them

Shomper and Courson also note that in fixed fee work it is important for all parties to be aware of the factors that increase cost, and to figure out how to control them. For example:

> If depositions are driving the cost of litigation, inside and outside counsel might consider whether fewer depositions can be taken. For example, some third-party witnesses could be interviewed, if willing, instead of deposed, with a resulting lower cost. The cost of depositions can be reduced by making an intelligent and informed analysis of the risk involved in not taking depositions of certain witnesses. Rather than turning over every stone in an effort to find every possible piece of relevant information, the client may be willing to take a small risk of an unpleasant surprise later in the litigation in exchange for cost savings now.

If simple specification of key cost factors can be added to the definition of a fixed fee, it will dramatically increase the chances of a mutually satisfactory outcome.

In addition, one of the most important steps in defining scope is clearly stating your assumptions at the outset. This takes some work and is so important that we have an entire section about it in the third edition of our *Legal Project Management Quick Reference Guide*.

Step 5. Set the price

Now the moment of truth: what will you charge for this work?

This is the most important step in fixed fee work, and the hardest.

When you are preparing a fixed fee bid, the most important goal is to win the work, while bidding a price that makes business sense for your firm. Unless you see the work as a loss leader that opens new doors, you must at least cover your costs. Starting out by estimating the hours the work will take is the key to doing this.

Chapters 6 and 7 in this book discuss several approaches to pricing. But ultimately there is only one way to get good at pricing: practice, practice, practice.

In a white paper entitled "Creating the Law Firm of the Future," Ralph Palumbo, founder of the Summit Law Group, has noted that:

> To be truly innovative, you have to learn to make your mistakes faster... every Summit lawyer has authority to propose any pricing system that the lawyer believes will match the Firm's incentives to the customer's goals. If an innovative pricing arrangement works well in one matter, we use it again. If a pricing arrangement doesn't work, we change it to one that does and don't repeat our mistake.[179]

So, at the end of the day, when you set a fixed fee, you will have to come up with your best guess, and move on. Then keep the agreement as simple as possible, because fixed price agreements work best in an atmosphere of trust.

Step 6. Protect yourself with a "safety valve" clause or change order

Sometimes things happen, and costs go up.

The traditional approach to this in most fields is to issue a change order in which both parties agree that the work went beyond the original scope and the client agrees to pay additional costs. Needless to say, this often requires some negotiation.

It can also be helpful to set an upper boundary "safety valve" that defines the maximum amount of work that will be delivered within the price.

For example, suppose a firm defines a fixed price of $30,000 for a matter that you predict will require 100 hours of work at an average rate of $300. Add a clause that says both parties agree that no more than 150 hours will be delivered for the $30,000. If the hours exceed 150, both parties agree to renegotiate the price.

That protects the firm from charging less than $200 per hour ($30,000 for 150 hours) in the absolute worst case, and also gives the client motivation to avoid unreasonable requests. When a project is bid, it also has a powerful psychological effect, in that some clients will do the worst case math, and perceive the $200 per hour limit as the true cost.

As the project proceeds, it also takes most of the arguing out of change orders. Both the client and the law firm can review actual hours spent in each phase of the project, compare them to budgeted hours, and discuss what might be changed BEFORE a project goes over budget.

Step 7. Manage the work to a successful conclusion

With hourly billing, there is little need for efficient management. In fact, the less efficient you are, the more money you will make in the short run, as long as the client is willing to pay. But in fixed price work, it is absolutely urgent that matters be completed within budget. This requires effective communication and is a totally different mindset. Ultimately, this has the potential to change everything about the way law firms operate, including the idea of compensating lawyers for billing more hours.

Step 8. Review the results

The best way to learn how to do better in the future is to study the past. When you close each file, meet with all the lawyers who worked on the matter, and discuss how to do better the next time.

The templates we use in our coaching and training include detailed instructions for "lessons learned" sessions at the end of every significant matter. These go far beyond a financial review, and include client satisfaction, communication, scope management, reusable work product, and more.

When you do a financial review, you may find you've done better than you would have with hourly billing, or you may have done worse. But as long as you are covering your true costs of doing business, you will be better off in the long term. If alternative fees help you to keep clients loyal in a tough economic environment, you are winning.

About contingent fees

In contingency arrangements, fees depend on success. Of course, this approach has long been used by plaintiffs' lawyers, but it is now becoming more common for the defense.

For example, Duane Morris billed on a contingency basis when it defended Eli Lilly in a $1.4-billion whistle blower suit over allegations of improper marketing of an anti-psychotic drug. An online account of that suit noted that:

> For at least the last decade, [Duane Morris] has focused about four to five percent of its billable time on contingency fee or other matters with alternative billing structures. And throughout that time it has cultivated a process for assessing risk and potential rewards. The firm will only take large commercial cases with a minimum fee of $1 million. There must be a 75% probability of success as determined by the firm's

> attorneys and contingent fee committee, and an opportunity to get three times the firm's recorded time.[180]

In the article, "Alternative Fees for Litigation: Improved Control and Higher Value," James Shomper and Gardner Courson list a variety of ways of defining success for contingent fees, including:

> Time of disposition (for example, dismissal or settlement by a specified date), type of disposition (summary judgment, voluntary dismissal), favorable judicial rulings (for example, denial of class certification, forum non conveniens, statute of limitations, preemption, or other dispositive rulings), disposition before fees and costs reach a specified level, and the like.[181]

Some clients have developed complex models to mathematically tie rewards to success, notably FMC Technologies' Alliance Counsel Engagement System (ACES). Alternative fees guru Jeff Carr, FMC's general counsel, "has increasingly applied the ACES model to all outside legal matters [at FMC Technologies] since... 2001."[182] In one example:

> The company withholds a portion of the fees incurred by the law firm and at the end of a predetermined period or the conclusion of the matter, the company conducts a performance appraisal of the work done by the law firm.... The law firm is rated from one to five with five being the highest score on a number of predetermined criteria. If the law firm scores "average," or a three, then the company pays the withheld amounts. If the law firm performs better than average, then the law firm receives a corresponding premium on the amount withheld. If the law firm scores lower than a three on the performance

> evaluation, then it receives a reduced amount on the amount withheld.

One ACC Docket article on this even includes tables showing how the math worked for a number of matters handled by Littler Mendelson. One table shows their ratings on six scales from an actual matter: understood goals, expertise, efficiency, responsiveness, predictive accuracy, effectiveness. It also shows how those numbers were used to calculate a 1.67% premium on the final fee for that matter.

However, from the law firm perspective, contingencies are becoming less attractive in today's cut-throat environment. According to one participant in our AmLaw 100 survey of alternative fees:

> Part of the difficulty of doing contingency work is that it makes the most sense for large law firms where there is a potential for a substantial recovery. But what we're seeing now is clients asking for a contingency where the amount you recover if you're successful is about equal to what you have invested in the matter. That's not a win-win, that's just a risk-risk. And those don't make sense.[183]

Value adjustment line

You won't find "value adjustment line" in anyone's list of the most common types of AFAs, because it is rather unusual. But it is worth discussing here because it represents a radical extreme in contingency thinking: legal matters are billed in the traditional hourly way, but at the end of the matter the client is invited to subtract or to add any amount, in order to reflect the value received.

Valorem Law Group, a Chicago litigation boutique, offers this explanation on its web page:

> On each bill, you have the right to make any adjustment to our proposed fee that you feel is needed. We provide value or you adjust the bill, it's that simple.
>
> We do this to give you the ultimate check on our unwavering commitment to client service, and to eliminate the concern that our level of service will wane once the work we've performed exceeds a given flat rate or capped fee allotment.
>
> Some have said that the Value Adjustment Line is extremely risky. We agree. If we aren't willing to risk our own fees on our service, do you really want us advocating for you?[184]

This is indeed risky, and it is hard to imagine a large firm successfully using this approach. But in his article "Creating the Law Firm of the Future," Ralph Palumbo, who originated the concept, reports that it has worked quite well with his boutique firm, Summit Law Group:

> Our experience with value-adjusted fees has been terrific. Our customers have voluntarily paid us tens and

> even hundreds of thousands of dollars more than our proposed fee in matters where the value of our product substantially exceeded the fee proposed. Other customers have asked us to raise our hourly rates in order to better reflect our value. We even benefit when a customer discounts our proposed fee (a rare event) because we get immediate notice that something is wrong and we have time to fix the problem and save the customer relationship.
>
> An unexpected benefit of our value-based pricing is that it has significantly reduced our accounts receivable. We get our bills out by the tenth of every month and ask to be paid promptly. Most of our customers respond—we believe in part because it's hard to object to paying a fee that the customer can adjust to any amount the customer believes fairly reflects value.[185]

Palumbo says that one key to success was building this approach into the firm's culture:

> No lawyer or staff member wants to be embarrassed by having a customer significantly reduce our proposed fee. The result is that our lawyers take more care to work with customers at the beginning of the engagement to define the scope and cost of the legal product to be provided. And they take more care to ensure that the cost of our legal product matches the customer's objectives.

Chapter 10

Conservative vs. aggressive approaches to AFAs

One of the most striking findings in the *LegalBizDev Survey of Alternative Fees* was the fact that firms offer AFAs with radically different business models. Some firms are aggressively bidding alternative fees to seek new business and are willing to risk lower profits to establish leadership positions in this growing market. Other firms are taking a much more conservative approach and try to assure that each deal is profitable on its own merits.

Conservative risk avoidance

Conservative firms are trying to plan bids so that every single AFA deal is profitable. In its most extreme form, this leads firms to seek and accept relatively little alternative fee work. One participant explained his firm's philosophy this way:

> Our firm is large enough to take some risks, but we're very fiscally conservative. We set aside a relatively low percentage of the accrual revenue of the department each year, [to] devote to these kinds of [alternative] arrangements. That way, we could tell the stewards of

> the firm—the executive committee, the chairman and anybody else who wanted to know—that we weren't going hog wild.

Traditionally, many law firms have expected to be paid a premium to assume risk. Of course, that drives up the price of fixed fee work and can scare clients off. Here is an example from a few years ago, before legal competition became fierce:

> A general counsel of a real estate company sent out RFPs to 50 law firms to solicit fixed fee bids in the areas of work that [the firms] regularly performed for the company. After analyzing the responses, he concluded that the fixed fee approach would actually cost the company 30% more than the traditional hourly rate approach. The likely reason for that result was that the law firms didn't have an accurate way of estimating potential costs (lack of data), and they did not want to take a risk. As a result, most estimates were 30%, or more, higher than the client perceived necessary or appropriate.

Despite the changes in the competitive environment, many of the lawyers we talk to today still believe that such premiums are necessary and appropriate. Here's what two of them said in our survey:

> If a law firm prepares a fixed price bid carefully and correctly, the client will often end up with a higher fee, since the law firm is taking additional risk. Businesses expect to be rewarded for taking risks.

> To be successful, any partnership must be a win-win, where everyone is taking risks and sharing rewards. If it's too one-sided, [then] it's not a partnership.

When I asked one survey participant what percent of the risk his firm was willing to bear, he said that, "law firms shouldn't take [more than] 50% of the risk. I think that's too high."

Clients may disagree about the exact percentage, but they certainly feel that law firms should share in the risk.

DuPont has led the movement to change the legal service model for nearly 20 years, and has more experience with alternative fees than most large corporate buyers. When DuPont held a conference for its outside counsel, an article describing the meeting reported that much of the discussion focused on risk:

> "Law firms... must be willing to put some skin in the game," said Silvio DeCarli, DuPont's chief litigation counsel. Too often, DuPont gets alternative fee proposals in which a firm makes money if the company loses a case, and even more money if the company wins. "Law firms too often get the idea that they've got to make money on everything, and a lot of it," DeCarli said. "And that's the tension."[186]

As Valorem's Patrick Lamb has noted, when law firms bid on fixed fees, many start by calculating a predicted "cost" based on the number of hours they expect the matter will require, at their standard hourly rates. But those rates already have a substantial profit margin built in. Then the firms increase the bid, to protect against contingencies. The result is a fixed price bid which is heavily weighted in the firm's favor.

Fred Bartlit, co-founder of Bartlit Beck, has compared this risk-averse mentality to oil companies that invest millions in drilling new wells, knowing from the start that many of those investments will turn out to be worthless "dry holes." But, as Bartlit has put it, "At Big Law, there's no such thing as a dry hole." Large firm lawyers expect to make a profit on every single matter, because every hour is billed to the client. Clients may win or lose, but their lawyers always win.

Just as oil companies must accept the fact that they may invest millions drilling for oil where there is none, Bartlit says that law firms must accept the fact that in order to win big you have to be willing and able to sometimes lose.

You would think that if anyone understood the need to take risks, it would be the law firms that have been working for DuPont for years. But even at DuPont's conference for outside counsel there was a split of opinions: "Who covers costs when a case takes an unexpected turn was a subject of debate. At the conference, some outside counsel said companies have an obligation to ensure their firms don't lose money if a turn of events isn't due to the firm's negligence. Other outside counsel said it's a risk law firms have to live with."[187]

Aggressive risk-taking

While some firms continue to take a conservative approach, others have been aggressively cutting prices and assuming risk for years.

A few years ago, in a panel I conducted on AFAs for Westlaw, Womble Carlyle partner Rob Fields argued that fees "must be transparent so the client can see that they won and they can defend the cost to their business people," and also said that "the client needs to win on every fee, every time, even though at larger law firms it's difficult to wrap our minds around this."

This comment led to a spirited exchange on Legal OnRamp, a private collaboration website for "in-house counsel and invited outside lawyers and third party service providers" about the wisdom of this approach. Some lawyers asked exactly how

Womble Carlyle structured fees to assure clients "winning every time."

Naturally, law firms do not want to publicize the details of their pricing tactics to competitors. But Womble Carlyle's Chief Client Development Officer Steve Bell did describe Fields' approach to an engagement where the fee was calculated three different ways and the client got to choose the lowest of the three for each matter:

> [The fee is calculated as] an hourly fee, a fixed fee and a productivity/results based fee. The lawyer does not know which will come out lowest until the end, so all three aspects of the representation (cost, efficiency, results) have to be managed. The client wins because it has certainty about the maximum cost, and also pays the lowest cost. The client can use the fixed fee component to shop the representation against the budgets/fixed fees of other competitors. The client can also budget with confidence. Some lawyers win and some lawyers lose. Low cost efficient providers win. High cost inefficient providers lose. (This result is Economics 101.) The first two components (hourly and fixed fee) are easy. The third component (productivity/results) is what is hard and new for both law firms and clients. It is also the key to the success of this approach because it is the source of the lawyer's incentive to provide good results.

Will this work in the long run? Of course no one knows. But if I could buy stock in law firms, I'd invest my money in the ones that are focused on maximizing client satisfaction for the lowest possible cost.

In the *LegalBizDev Survey of Alternative Fees*, some participants described a similarly aggressive approach: "I used to work in a venture capital firm, and I enjoy taking an entrepreneurial approach to betting on alternative fees. It's a portfolio; I don't need to win every one. If I make 20 bets and five are disastrous but three are home runs, I will do very well. If I try to engineer these arrangements so I can't lose, I'll never win the big ones."

Aggressive firms stress the value of building long-term relationships with key clients. "We've had situations in corporate deals where we've really gotten burned on something, but if it's a good client, they don't say "gotcha" and laugh about the fact that you made a bad deal. They say that we'll do more deals [in the future] and life goes on, and we assume that we'll make it up in volume by being engaged in better situations."

Aggressive firms have also actively jumped in to do more alternative fee deals, even when it meant they had to pay a price and learn by doing. "One way [to deal with uncertainty] is to wait until all of the questions are answered and then act when and if the sea change occurs. The other way, which is what our firm is doing, is to 'just do it,' proactively seeking engagements from clients with value-based alternative fee arrangements even when it's hard to quantify costs. We plan to step out there and take the risk."

Differences of opinion about shadow billing

Firms were also split in our survey on "shadow billing," in which law firms that are billing an AFA continue to provide information about what the costs would have been if matters were billed hourly.

Aggressive firms believe that this openness and transparency will serve as the basis of a partnership. If both parties see where things really stand, they can renegotiate in good faith if costs are either higher or lower than what both parties expected.

On the other side, conservative firms resist client pressures to provide this information, for fear that it will be used against them. A deal is a deal in this approach, and the client should not get to look behind the curtain to see whether the firm has won or lost.

A number of participants in our survey were strongly opposed to shadow billing:

> If we really want to get alternative fees into the psyche of both clients and lawyers, we need to stop clients from measuring how much more the firm made than their hourly rate, and we need to get lawyers away from thinking about how much they earned less than their hourly rate. Someone's got to say "Look, I did a job for you. I collected five million dollars. Was it worth it?" Yes or no?
>
> In some cases, what's happening is that even when there's an agreement that the fixed fee is going to be allowed, the client wants to reconcile the time that's put into it and see if they got a good deal or a bad deal. And as long as that's the kind of relationship it is, it really isn't an alternative billing arrangement. "Did I do better or worse than under the old system?" If general counsel really want to get rid of the billable hour system for billing, then you can't have all these post-audit questions about it. If you agree on something, and there's value, and we found a way to staff it differently, we should benefit from those efforts.

Some experts from the client side are also opposed to shadow billing. According to Mike Roster, co-chair of the ACC Value Challenge committee:

> Shadow hours are lose-lose. If the success of an AFA is based upon a comparison with shadow hours, the only

successful AFA will be one that comes in at exactly the same price as the matter would have cost with traditional hours. If the shadow hours are less than the client paid, the client feels it got a bad deal, and if the shadow hours come in higher, then the firm will conclude the matter under an AFA was not profitable.

Equally if not more important, shadow hours take both the firm's and the client's attention away from what should be their focus: reducing cost, providing near certainty in cost, and improving outcomes. If the targets are achieved, the client should have no care whatsoever about what shadow hours would have cost. That's when the client starts to make substantial gains as the firm maintains and even improves profitability.

On the other side of the argument, some aggressive firms allow and even encourage shadow billing. As one survey participant put it, "If we hide things like [hours], it's not going to work. We're interested in this from a partnership perspective. There has to be mutual trust. If [clients] think we're just doing this and reaping in additional money, it's not going to work."

Some deals also include a formal or informal "true-up," a process in which actual hourly costs are compared to fixed prices from time to time, and adjustments are made to bring the two in line.

It is important to note that the argument over shadow billing is taking place in an age of transparency, in which business leaders preach the value of openness, honesty and accountability and even top-secret government documents sometimes find their way to the web.[188]

In this environment, some lawyers have concluded that it does not matter whether shadow billing is good or bad. It is inevitable, so you may as well get used to it.

Chapter 11
Using AFAs to develop new business

When ALM Legal Intelligence asked law firms why they offered AFAs, their top reason by far was marketing.[189] Ninety-one percent of the firms in this survey reported that they used AFAs to "attract and maintain clients."

This chapter begins with a description of how AFAs are being used to build new business at six leading firms. This is followed by a discussion of the benefits of a proactive approach in AFA marketing.

Examples of AFA marketing

While some firms are just starting to use AFAs, others have been using them to develop new business for quite a while. According to Peter Kalis, the chairman and managing partner of K&L Gates, a global firm with nearly 2,000 lawyers, "We have offered alternative fees for more than 20 years... We were dragged there kicking and screaming by a few key clients who led this trend, including DuPont and United Technologies. We found to our amazement that it was a really good way to do business, both for us and for the client."

Adams and Reese, a firm with 13 offices throughout the southern United States, began offering AFAs for the same reason. The firm encountered several situations "where we wouldn't get the work unless we agreed to a flat fee or fixed fee," according to firm-wide managing partner Chuck Adams. For example:

> We work with one global company that requires standard trademark and patent services in a number of foreign countries, and we do all of their intellectual property work for a flat fee. We trust them, at their full discretion, to pay us a bonus at the end of each year if they think they're getting value. The agreement gets renewed every year, and they do treat us fairly.
>
> We have relationships with some companies that have a large number of fairly similar transactions. We represent entities that buy hundreds of thousands of acres of timberland and they have a volume of fairly similar sales of smaller parcels. When there's a closing, it becomes pretty much a commodity, a fairly standard transaction. We have arrangements with a number of clients like this to handle things on a pure flat fee arrangement.

These types of arrangements work best, Adams noted, when one "has a good prior relationship with a client. We understand how they do business and what they need, and are therefore able to price it in a reasonable way."

Joseph E. Mais, firm-wide chair of commercial litigation at Perkins Coie, a firm with over 850 lawyers in 19 offices in the US and Asia, made a similar point in discussing his firm's approach to AFAs: "They require a fair amount of trust. They also require significant knowledge of the client's business to be priced and staffed appropriately." For this reason, Mais says, it's easier to offer AFAs to existing clients when there is a mutual understanding than to new clients who are unknown.

Like K&L Gates and Adams and Reese, Perkins Coie first started offering AFAs due to client demands. In fact, Mais identified two categories of work in which "if we weren't prepared to offer AFAs, we wouldn't be getting hired for a significant portion of the work"—the representation of policyholders in insurance coverage work, and patent work in which the firm represents defendants who are sued by non-practicing entities. The coverage work is generally done on a partial contingent fee basis—a monthly rate with a success fee. In the patent sphere, says Mais, "the predominant AFA model is a fee cap, hopefully coupled with success fees."

In some cases, AFAs have also proven useful in attracting new clients. For example, "In multi-party cases, one or more defendants might seek to join forces with a longstanding client, where everyone believes there can be efficiency in having a single law firm dealing with common issues. Here, we have had a fair amount of success bringing in new clients on an alternative fee basis when they weren't our primary relationship at the start."

At Crowell & Moring, a firm with nearly 500 lawyers in eight offices, Kathy Kirmayer, chair of the D.C. litigation group and a member of the firm's finance and AFAs committees, notes, "We have been using AFAs for more than a decade and don't view them as 'alternative' because we think they provide value that far exceeds just the bottom line." The firm has refined another innovative technique for using AFAs to bring in new clients with a type of antitrust proposal that is unusual for a large corporate firm.

When a corporation pleads guilty to some sort of antitrust violation, Kirmayer says, Crowell & Moring lawyers often identify not only firm clients that have purchased significant amounts of the product that has been subject to price-fixing or similar conduct, but sometimes companies new to the firm as well. Those purchasers will usually have the right to sue the antitrust violator for money damages, and verdicts or settlements can run into the tens or hundreds of millions of dollars.

Crowell & Moring's "recovery practice" represents purchasers for a contingent fee—a percentage of the amount it is able to recover for the client. This has been very appealing for new clients of the firm, Kirmayer says, and several clients that established their relationship for this type of work later have grown their relationship with the firm in other practice areas for work on non-contingency matters.

This practice started more than a decade ago when some existing corporate clients sought counsel from the firm, saying they had been victimized by antitrust conspiracies, and asked the firm to represent them. Then Crowell & Moring expanded the practice to serve existing clients and to cultivate new ones, which it sees as an investment in the future.

"We are really in this in order solve the immediate problem for the client and then to develop them into institutional clients of the firm," Kirmayer says. "We want to demonstrate what kind of lawyers we are, beyond these antitrust cases." Although antitrust is the core of the recovery practice, Kirmayer says that Crowell & Moring has expanded it for trade and customs duty cases, intellectual property, and tax matters as well.

Jonathan Cooper, a partner at the Cleveland office of Tucker Ellis, also reports that AFAs have been an excellent way to attract new business for his firm.

One technique that Tucker Ellis has used is to bill a fixed sum on a quarterly or monthly basis for all legal work of a given nature such as tort defense or employment litigation. These arrangements often include a risk collar. If the actual hourly cost proves to be less than the agreed upon fee, the client and the firm split the savings 50/50. If the actual hourly cost exceeds the fixed price, the client pays half of the overage, and the firm pays the other half. "This mitigates both risk and reward and provides incentives and openness between the lawyer and the client," Cooper says.

For example, Tucker Ellis used this type of arrangement to get some mass tort work from one large state by agreeing to a fixed quarterly payment with a risk collar. "The client's associate general counsel was dissatisfied with her previous law firm because of uncertainty about the fees," Cooper recalls. "She loved this new approach. Many clients think lawyers are just trying to bill as much as possible to rip them off, and this clearly wasn't the case with us."

In another type of arrangement, Tucker Ellis approached a client that had been on the wrong side of a multi-million dollar verdict, and asked to handle the appeal in exchange for a percentage of the amount that the client would save if the appeal were successful. "This worked well. We thought there was a high chance of winning the appeal. The client got a top-flight appellate lawyer, and the incentive was running the client's way," Cooper says.

At Warner Norcross & Judd, senior partner J.A. Cragwall, Jr. has found that AFAs have been equally attractive to their clients. In one case, the Michigan firm was competing for a large chunk of national business litigation for a Fortune 500 manufacturer. Also in the running, Cragwall says, were other major firms from money centers such as New York, Chicago, Cleveland, and Milwaukee.

Cragwall reports that Warner Norcross was able to get the work, and develop an ongoing relationship with this major company, by "working up a budget, and then proposing to bill the client for a portion of the budget each month." If the matter were resolved earlier than planned, the law firm would split the savings with the client. That way, Cragwall says, "The client may get a surprise, but it's a good surprise."

This particular client, Cragwall explained, felt that the best way to get a handle on spiraling legal costs was to "control cycle time—the time that it takes to finish a matter." The firm's alternative fee proposal responded directly to that concern.

At the Jackson, Mississippi, office of Butler Snow, Partner Charles Johnson III says alternative fees "have become a standard way of doing business for us. We have some clients who prefer hourly billing, but more and more of our clients want and expect predictability."

Johnson says that in the past five years, for example, Butler Snow has begun to do all the nationwide product liability work for a global top 20 pharmaceutical firm by offering alternative fees. In addition, the firm has been able to land a considerable amount of transactional and contract review work for that client by using its experience to accurately estimate how much time each task will take.

"For these deals, we are now able to offer a fixed fee for due diligence and advance work, another fixed fee for the drafting and negotiating process until closing, and another fixed fee for closing and post-closing work," Johnson says.

All of the firms described in this chapter, and many others, have found that AFAs can help bring in new business.

Some firms aggressively promote AFAs. Others, like K&L Gates, describe their approach as "agnostic." According to Chairman Kalis:

> For some clients, it's a requirement to use AFAs. For others, it's an arrow in our marketing quiver. We shoot it a lot, and some clients duck and others welcome it... We're happy to offer AFAs and happy to go hourly... We truly don't have a preference... Our historical client base consists of extraordinarily sophisticated consumers of legal services. When they are able to engage in an informed dialogue with a provider of legal services on a subject near and dear to them, that is always a positive step in the relationship.

In general, Kalis says that the AFA movement has been "a healthy development in our profession. I think it's a sign of the maturation of the industry, that law firms and clients are having more informed discussions about the cost of legal services than they did 10 years ago."

In addition, "AFAs are a great tool for helping law firms meet client needs in a way that furthers the relationship," according to Chuck Adams of Adams and Reese.

> But the most successful ones develop from existing client relationships because clients and lawyers must be in synch. It is critical to understand clients' expectations, their philosophical approach. Do they want to turn over every rock, for example, or just the basics? Lawyers can eliminate inefficiency, and staff and price AFAs best when they understand this and there is a relationship of mutual trust.

"It can be complicated to work these things out," according to Perkins Coie's Mais. "But my guess is that AFAs will grow as big companies continue to converge on using fewer law firms and developing deeper relationships with their lawyers."

The 194 law firms in the *ALM Legal Intelligence Survey* agree: 82% expect the volume of AFAs to increase over the next five years.

To assure that this trend works out for both clients and their firms, Mais says, "the most important core principle for AFA success is to align the firm's interest with the client's interest."

Proactive AFA marketing

While some firms talk to clients about AFAs only when they have to, others proactively start the discussion themselves. In our *LegalBizDev Survey of Alternative Fees*, several senior decision makers stressed the value of a proactive approach in which discussing AFAs is part of the selling process. "We are talking to our long-time clients and proactively letting them know that if they want to discuss alternative fee arrangements, our firm is interested, willing, and capable to talk about such arrangements. We want to open the lines of communication, so we're talking to all our clients about this all the time, [and] I know other firms are doing that to my clients, too."

Other participants in our survey talked about how they actively used AFAs to take clients away from their competitors:

> One of the things that we're seeing with this new paradigm [is that] everybody's clients are potential prey, or at risk. For example, say I've been doing a small amount of work for a big Fortune 500 client that I'd really like to do more work for… I will go to them and say, "You know what? I know you're using Acme law firm to do this work. If you will give me some information about how much you've spent over the past five years on that type of work, I'll give you a fixed fee proposal for all that work that will provide you with

> certainty and predictability with top-notch legal talent. We'd love to do that work for you."

A proactive discussion of AFAs can have valuable marketing benefits, even when a client stays with hourly billing. "Despite the fact that many clients ultimately decide to stay with hourly rates, we will always explore alternative fee options in depth at their request. At least half the time, they will come back to us with new work."

That is not to say that it is easy to offer winning AFA bids. One CFO in our survey offered a rather jaundiced view of "the product" his lawyers are offering:

> One of the problems is that our partners seem to think they have a better product than the people we're competing with. And so when the client compares our fixed fee to other firms', they ask how come we can't do the work for less. [The partners typically reply that competitors are] not offering the same product that we are, so I ask [the partners], "Why are we offering a product that the client is not willing to pay for?" It's a whole mindset which will require time to change.

At the end of the day, it will take time to make the transition to AFAs, and there will be winners and losers. As one AmLaw 100 decision maker summed it up in our survey: "This is hard. Partners will have difficulty embracing this sort of change."

Chapter 12
Putting it all together

Throughout this book, we have talked about the complex interrelations between legal project management and pricing. The need for change in these areas is easiest to see when lawyers are working on AFAs.

AFAs and pricing

Traditionally, some firms have had little central control over client matters, and individual lawyers have struck their own deals. It was only when AFAs began to spread that this was perceived as a problem. As one respondent in the *LegalBizDev Survey of Alternative Fees* put it, "until recently, [alternative fees have] been done very much on an *ad hoc* basis, sometimes even under the radar screen. People were doing things on an alternative fee basis and we didn't even know that it was happening."

But now that volume is increasing, many firms are trying to bring the process under central control. "What we're trying to do now, as we see demand in the marketplace going up, is bring a much more organized and thoughtful approach to alternative fees."

The centralized pricing director approach described in Chapter 7 is one way of doing this, but there are many other approaches to improved pricing, such as:

> Proposals involving fixed or contingent fees are reviewed by the new business committee, which has a telecon at 9 AM every day and normally makes decisions on the same day.
>
> We have an Alternative Fee Arrangements Committee... that includes representatives from our Client Relations Group, our Accounting Group, our Information Technologies Group and also different practice group leaders. And we've created a structure for getting these alternative billing arrangements approved quickly and efficiently.
>
> Our firm has an 11-page chart summarizing what types of fees have worked in the past, and why. [It also summarized] the structure we used, [and] how it worked out.
>
> Our firm has identified four senior partners in four different areas as "alternative fee czars" who serve as a clearinghouse for alternative fee proposals that come in from our attorneys.

Some firms established systems years ago to collect pricing information and distribute it to partners:

> In our Labor and Employment Practice Group, we've been using task-based and activity-based codes for 15 or 20 years, ever since they came out from the ABA. Like everybody else, we bill by the tenth of the hour. And next to every hour's entry, [the lawyer enters] a task-based code and an activity-based code that describes what they were doing. In every case that I've had for the

> last 15 years, I could go back and find out how much it cost to do a summary judgment in that kind of case. I can follow that same process for plaintiff depositions, class certification, and every other phase of a piece of litigation. This information has been invaluable to our Labor and Employment Group in completing fixed fee estimates.

The same participant went on to explain that other practice groups in his firm have taken another approach:

> Some of the other practice groups didn't feel the need to use task-based billing codes, because clients weren't asking for it and because it's extra work. So we decided that we needed to reverse-engineer some cases. In each of our practice groups, we went back and chose a number of differentiated types of cases. [One group we selected was] our Intellectual Property and Technology Group. Examples included a soft IP case, a hard IP case and a patent prosecution matter. We tore those bills apart and applied them to a standardized budget template. We created what the budget would have looked like [by] reverse-engineering the bills to come up with those estimates. As we do this work across the firm, we continually develop a better sense of what it costs to complete specific portions of representations.

AFAs and LPM

AFAs clearly require lawyers to learn new skills in project planning and management. Anyone who has ever read a book on project management understands the need to define scope clearly and then manage staff to stay within budget. But participants in our survey reported that for many lawyers who have spent their entire career billing by the hour, it is uncharted territory:

> Lawyers are not known for being the greatest project management folks in the world. If they are going to try alternative billing methods, they have to be able to deliver what they are offering. This is a fundamental change in the industry, and lawyers will have to improve their project management skills in order to succeed in this area.
>
> When I first started working for this law firm… I asked, "What's your methodology?" and they said, "What's a methodology?" The idea runs against lawyers' DNA. They see every deal as customized and unique.
>
> It's a lot easier to come up with an alternative fee than it is to teach somebody to project-manage.

Each of the eight key issues in legal project management which we discussed in Chapter 3 came up in survey comments, starting with defining and managing scope:

> Lawyers and their clients will need to learn to be more careful and disciplined about making fee deals: defining scope, managing changes in scope, dealing with changed circumstances, dealing with the impact of client delay and whole contractual terms and managing the contractual relationships.

> The best project managers I have seen understand that some give and take [is needed]. An ability to reach quick and practical agreements is far preferable to a consistently contentious relationship which generally increases costs and produces unsatisfactory results.

When scope is clearly defined in the first place, it is much easier to stay within budget. And when things change, as they inevitably will, it also makes it easier to talk frankly and openly with the client about what course to take, and how this will affect cost. "If the assumption is we were supposed to review 60,000 documents, [but] then we had to review 200,000 documents, it offers an opportunity to sit down with the client and ask how we can handle this work that is outside the scope."

Managing client relationships begins with communication, and this is particularly vital when it comes to change orders—formal agreements that the scope of a project has changed in a way that also changes the budget:

> The communication aspect between a partner and the client as the deal progresses is very important. You can't wait until the end to talk about all the change orders. You really can't be afraid to address these issues, [and] a lot of partners [are].
>
> The American Institute of Architects has a standard form for a written change order if you change a design [during a construction project]. But I deal with partners all the time, [who] say that they changed something and that the client acknowledged the change. I ask, "Is it written anywhere?" And the answer is no.

Budgeting also came up early and often in our interviews. "When you go to these other types of arrangements—fixed fees, partial fixed fees, contingent fees, partial contingent fees—it becomes imperative to keep track of [budgets]. [Lawyers] don't know how to do that [and] they don't want to do that. And truthfully, our systems make it hard to do that."

A solid budget starts by assigning the right people to the team. "We really need to manage the matters much more closely than we ever did before [to] make sure that they're being staffed and handled efficiently. Clients don't want new lawyers working on their matters. Rather than have a first-year associate spend 10 hours researching something, they'd rather have a senior partner spend half an hour and solve the problem."

Once the right people are on the team, they must be managed in a way that lawyers have traditionally ignored:

> For alternative billing to be successful for both the client and law firm, the partners have to re-think their approach and try to decide the most efficient way to approach matters. For example, instead of sending an associate off to research 50 issues that could come up in a litigation, you might focus strictly on the small number of issues that are likely to be most important.
>
> The more aggressive a bid is, the more pressure there is on the lawyers managing the matter to be efficient and to staff the matter at the lowest possible level. The pressure is a good thing. It forces lawyers to take a hard look at costs and benefits. Is it really necessary to proofread that agreement eight times?

If alternative fees are to work well in the future, inside and outside counsel must learn how to collaborate to improve efficiency, and both must manage matters in new ways:

> [When working on hourly projects] you see inside counsel wanting to drive how the matter is managed. "No, we're not going to draft this now," or "Yes, I want it revised today, even though we haven't gotten all the

> input from the various other parties," kind of micro-managing the process itself. If we're to learn to be more efficient... we need to be able to control how we do that. And just like it's going to be really hard for our partners to let go of the old ways, I suspect it will [also] be hard for inside counsel to let go.
>
> It is very difficult for a law firm to tell a client that a matter is not going well from a cost or process point of view because of what is going on in the legal department.
>
> I'm working with a very large client on coming up with a good menu of alternative plans, but I've been working on it for quite a while with the GC and we haven't gotten very far yet. I'm reluctant to tell him that his own people cause a fair amount of inefficiency, because he's not going to want to hear it.

Summing it all up, one participant put it like this: "We need to be better managers of what we do for clients. If law firms do not take the lead in getting clear agreements with clients about the work we are expected to do, what the client will be doing, and then manage our resources carefully to meet those agreements, we will be doing the same work for a lot less net income."

Chapter 13
What should you do?

An ounce of application is worth a ton of abstraction.

– Booker T. Washington

There is no question that LPM, new approaches to pricing, and AFAs are changing the legal landscape. The only question is: what are you going to do about it?

This chapter lists 10 recommendations, based on what successful law firms have learned to date.

1. Don't overanalyze; just do it

Law firms tend to make decisions by committee, which is a great way to delay or avoid decisions. In a volatile marketplace, the firms that act quickly, take risks, and learn from experience will win.

2. Ask clients what they want

Get out of the office, and talk to your top clients. Listen. Give them what they want and need. If you don't talk to your clients about these issues, someone else will.

3. Identify internal champions

Some lawyers will be more enthusiastic than others about this approach, and some will be better than others at planning bids and managing projects. They should be given the support they need, and their success should be publicized.

4. Get off to a good start

You won't get a second chance to make a first impression, and if the first program for your group is not well designed and executed, it may be quite some time before there is a second one.

5. Increase efficiency by adapting tools from other professions

Learn from other industries and professions by borrowing tactics they have developed from decades of experience bidding, planning and managing work to maximize efficiency and quality.

6. Define and measure success

Some projects will be much more successful than others. You need to be able to quickly identify the winners and losers, so that you can refine your tactics and increase your success rate. In the early stages, measurement should probably be limited to the subjective reaction of participants, and the extent to which they continue to apply key concepts with their clients. As your projects become more sophisticated, consider tracking more formal measures of success, such as:

- Client satisfaction
- Repeat business
- AFA profitability
- Realization
- Percent of lawyers who establish a budget before each matter over $x, a threshold that fits your group
- Percent of lawyers who report actual costs vs. planned costs, at least once a month and preferably more often

7. Evaluate results regularly, and learn from mistakes

Once standards have been set, key people within the firm can evaluate results quarterly or on another schedule, to see what works and what doesn't. In this new, more challenging, world, it is not possible to avoid occasional failures. But it is essential to learn from mistakes and to improve results.

8. Tie results to compensation

The hardest part of this new environment will be making money. The second-hardest part will be splitting it up. After several decades of working with a number of systems for compensating my own employees and studying compensation systems at other firms, I believe that there is only one sure-fire way to make any individual happy with a compensation system: pay them more than everyone else.

This is especially troubling in partnerships where relative contributions are controversial and where it is very easy for unhappy rainmakers to take their clients to other firms.

As Susan Hackett wrote in the article *Six Critical Strategies Used By Law Firm Pricing Directors*, "It is especially important to consider the connection between pricing policies and compensation. Lawyers must begin to understand that what they're being paid more dollars to provide is not a larger stack of hours, but a larger profit margin or a more cost-effective service delivery mechanism, or improved client satisfaction and repeating business."[190]

It is easy to predict that compensation will remain a source of controversy, especially for firms whose total revenues are shrinking. But as the world becomes more competitive, it will become increasingly important to assure that the greatest rewards are given to the people who are most responsible for the firm's success, and that everyone understands how such decisions are made.

9. Don't be penny wise and pound foolish

As the owner of a firm that provides consulting to law firms, I can hardly claim to be an unbiased observer on the matter of law firm spending. But some of the decisions you make in this area may affect the very survival of your firm. Therefore, prudent firms will recognize the need to invest in this area.

10. Act like an entrepreneur, not like a lawyer

It is a mistake to approach pricing and AFAs like a lawyer, trying to craft perfect agreements and close all the loopholes. In a rapidly changing legal landscape, lawyers who insist on extensive analyses before taking any action risk being left behind. Approach each new matter like an entrepreneur who is willing to do whatever it takes to bring in new business and can't wait to get started.

Do these 10 recommendations sound like more than you can handle?

Then just focus on the first one. As Camden Webb, a partner at Williams Mullen, put it, "Don't hold a series of committee meetings for a year and then do a top-down analysis. Just do something. This will spread project management, because when lawyers succeed, others in the firm will imitate their success."

If you already know what that first "something" should be for your practice, try it. If you don't have a clear idea yet, scan this book to review what other firms are doing, and pick an idea that resonates with you. And get used to the idea that whatever you do, it is the proverbial first step in a thousand-mile journey.

No one knows how the changes in LPM, pricing and AFAs will affect law firms over the coming years and decades. The only way to find what works for you is to try it. When you win some, do more of that. When you lose some, accept it as the price of doing business.

Learn and adapt.

The sooner you start, the more likely you are to beat the competition.

Appendix
The mathematics of pricing

If you have reviewed the theory of pricing in Chapter 6 and now want to dig deeper into the numbers behind pricing decisions and profitability, you have come to the right section of the book.

Partner profits and client perceptions

In the May 2012 issue of *ACC Docket*, Markus Hartmann and Bill Mordan describe a new approach to billing they called the Litigation Investment Model.

"The concept is very simple," the authors say. "The law firm agrees to deduct a fixed percentage from their invoice—the same amount they would have earned as profit—and treat the deduction as an investment in the litigation. In return for that ongoing investment of their profit, the firm can earn a bonus depending on the total amount invested and the outcome of the case."[191]

The article includes several examples that use flat rate billing for phases. In the simplest, a firm is paid 70% of its normal fee as the case proceeds. The other 30%, representing the firm's potential profit, is invested in the outcome.

One example shows a case with an initial discovery phase that would have been billed at $500,000 if it were performed for a flat fee.[192] Of this, only $350,000 (70%) would be paid when the work is performed. The other $150,000 (30%) would be held back. At the end of the case, if the firm won, they would be paid double the hold back ($300,000). If they settled, they would be paid the exact amount that was held back ($150,000). If they lost, they would be paid nothing.

The actual multipliers are negotiated at the beginning of each case, based on a joint assessment of the facts of the case. Figure 4 in their article illustrates a more complex case with six possible outcomes, each with a different multiplier ranging from 0 to 2.5 (for an "exceptional case finding and award of attorney fees pursuant to 35 U.S.C 285").

According to the authors, the key difference from other alternative fee arrangements is that "While standard hold back agreements and success fees focus on the client's savings, the Litigation Investment Model focuses on something far more relevant: the firm's profit." In essence, they argue that law firms should only make a profit if they succeed in meeting the client's objectives.

From the in-house client's point of view, all this sounds quite reasonable. In most businesses, profit is a kind of bonus. It is what is left over after all expenses have been paid, the revenue a company receives over and above its breakeven point: money they "don't really need." In theory, companies could stay in business if they never made a profit and simply broke even forever.

The Merriam Webster dictionary defines profit as "the difference between the amount earned and the amount spent in buying, operating, or producing something." If that's the way law firms defined profit, this model might seem not only simple but also fair and reasonable. But, as explained in Chapter 7, law firm definitions of profit are far more complex and confusing.

In the *2012 Global Partner Compensation Survey*, Ed Wesemann and Nick Jarrett-Kerr reported an analysis of 263 large law firms in the United States, the United Kingdom, Europe, and Australia.[193] They classified compensation systems into seven categories: lockstep, equal distribution, modified lockstep, formula, combination, subjective, and corporate. The last of these, corporate, would make it easy to calculate profits since "partners receive a salary and bonus based on performance and then are paid dividends based on the profitability of the firm." There's just one problem: this corporate compensation system is "rarely seen in the US or Canada."

In the six systems which are widely used to compensate partners, the line between cost and profit ranges from fuzzy to non-existent.

In other businesses, when the finance department considers the price they should charge for a product, they pay special attention to the break-even point, the amount they must charge to cover their expenses before profit. When lawyers decide what to charge, most are blissfully unaware of their firm's break-even point. The CFO, the managing partner and other leaders probably have a good idea of the break-even point, but even that is not as unambiguous as in other businesses, because it is based on assumptions about what partners expect to be paid.

When Hartmann and Mordan used an estimated profit of 30% in their example, they explained in a footnote that they got this figure from the *American Lawyer's* widely publicized concept of "profits per partner," used in its annual rankings of the AmLaw 200. "Thanks to law firm bravado and their own published data," they said, "we have a pretty good idea of how much profit a large firm makes: about 38 percent, based on the published results of the top 200 firms in the United States."[194]

Unfortunately, the American Lawyer's definition of profit—"net operating income for the firm divided by the number of equity partners"—differs from both the dictionary definition and the normal usage of the word "profit" in other businesses. Net operating income is calculated by subtracting all of a firm's expenses from revenue **excluding partner compensation**. To put it another way, partners may get 100% of their pay from the pool of "profits per partner." They may also pay taxes and benefits from this pool. If those "profits" were permanently withheld, partners would be paid little or nothing for their work, and would certainly not consider themselves to be breaking even. They would be working for free.

When Hartmann and Mordan describe the Litigation Investment Model, it seems they recognize it is a bit one-sided when they call it "beneficial to the client and more comfortable to the law firm." They also note than when in-house lawyers negotiate these agreements, they should "expect an equity partner to be squeamish and uncertain."[195]

There are good business reasons for law firms to be reluctant to embrace the Litigation Investment Model. To see one reason why, consider the math for a hypothetical case handled by a three-lawyer firm, with two associates and one partner. Assume that the firm accepted the case on the Litigation Investment Model, and used the assumptions from the article that partner profits are 38%, and that 30% of revenue should be invested in the outcome of the case.

Here are some rounded figures showing what compensation for this firm might have looked like on a standard "bill as you go" agreement:

Partner compensation ("profits per partner")	38%	$380,000 ($300,000 salary plus 26.67% tax and benefits)
Overhead including rent and salaries of associates and staff	62%	$620,000
Total	100%	$1,000,000

Here is what happens to the partner's short-term pay if 30% is withheld until the end of the matter:

Profit invested in the case, paid or not paid at the end of the matter, depending on its outcome	30%	$300,000
Short-term partner compensation	8%	$80,000 ($63,200 salary plus approximately 26.67% tax and benefits)
Overhead including rent and salaries of associates and staff	62%	$620,000
Total	100%	$1,000,000

In other words, the partner's short-term salary was reduced from $300,000 to $63,200 after tax and benefits. Not many lawyers could easily take this kind of reduction and still pay their mortgage.

The thought that in the long term their salary could go back up to $300,000 if the case settled, or could double if they won the case, would take some of the sting out of the salary reduction. But they might still have trouble paying their bills in the short term. And if they lost the case, they would never recover the difference.

Of course, this type of salary reduction would not be necessary in a firm with 100 or 1,000 lawyers, because one lawyer's shortfall in income could be made up from the billings of other attorneys, just as they are in contingency cases. In essence, however, these larger firms would be robbing Peter to pay Paul.

The truth is, given thousands of simultaneous matters at a large firm, with different fee structures, time frames, payment schedules and realization rates, many firms have traditionally found it difficult to track the profitability of individual matters. According to the *2012 Altman Weil Law Firms in Transition Survey*, 17% of firms are "not sure" whether their AFAs are more or less profitable than hourly matters on the average.[196] So they certainly don't know how individual matters are doing.

Under the Litigation Investment Model, many lawyers will make less money.

Could lawyers protect their profitability by delivering the same quality for 30% fewer hours at the same average rate?

They might well be able to do so in some cases, but the answer obviously depends on the actual price. If the winning bid was calculated based on the fees charged several years ago, some lawyers could apply project management techniques and reduce the total hourly billings by that much, while still producing a similar result. But if the 100% price was based on a fiercely competitive bid, or a reverse auction, firms may have trouble breaking even with 100% of the price, much less with 70% of it.

At the end of the day, is the Litigation Investment Model a good way to compensate law firms?

According to Toby Brown, Director of Strategic Pricing and Analytics at Akin Gump, "Law firm profitability is so difficult to define that you could not really use it to calculate what you were willing to invest." More importantly, he continued, "This model assumes that risk sharing is the motivation behind alternative fees, and for many clients it is not." Brown's claim is supported by the results of a recent survey of ALM Legal Intelligence.[197] When 141 law departments were asked to identify the benefits of AFAs, only 35% named risk sharing. This came in fourth behind cost predictability/transparency (87%), cost savings (68%) and increased efficiency (44%).

Chris Ende, senior manager of project management and pricing at Goodwin Procter, also noted that even if risk sharing is the goal, "It shouldn't matter whether the fee structure is based on profit. Clients who want to align their interests with the law firms they engage should focus on what value the law firms provide—not just based on efficiency, but also on results. You can do a great job of pushing down legal fees, but if you end up having to pay out $10 million in damages, you lost."

Despite these objections, some in-house lawyers may find the Litigation Investment Model very attractive.

The general counsel who uses it could begin earning points with his management on day one by tying payment to success. It certainly pleased the CEO quoted by Hartmann and Mordan in their article: "I only get a bonus if I win in the marketplace. The same rules should apply to your law firms."[198]

Even if the law firm is ultimately paid exactly 100% of what it would have gotten when it billed hourly, 30% is paid at the end, so the client has much better cash flow at the law firm's expense.

If the client pays more than 100%, it will usually be because they saved more than that based on the outcome of the case.

From the law firm's point of view, the picture is less clear. The downside is certainly significant, and each firm will have to decide what cases make business sense at what prices. To do so, they will first need a much better understanding of their own costs, and the organizational discipline to avoid accepting cases that will benefit individual lawyers by keeping them working on billable matters, but reduce the average earnings of the rest.

From the profession's point of view, is this a sustainable way of doing business? Over the next few years, we may find out.

Some pricing formulas

Much of the concern about the litigation investment model results from confusion over the meaning of profit. Using a little bit of mathematical notation can help to clarify the situation here.

Recall the hypothetical case of solo practitioner Beth. As explained in Chapter 6, she hopes to bill for 2,000 hours in her first year, and would like to get started by at least keeping her $250,000 salary as a base. She has done a business plan and anticipates overhead of $100,000. Some simple math tells Beth that she can bill 2,000 hours at an average rate of $200 per hour, bring in $400,000 in revenue, pay herself a $250,000 salary and still make a profit. Here are the numbers again in a more systematic and mathematical form:

Variable	Description	Budget
S	Salary	$250,000
RH	Realized Hours	2,000
O	Overhead	$100,000
TE	Total Expense	$350,000
BR	Actual Hourly Billing Rate	$200
TR	Total Revenue = $RH \cdot BR$	$400,000
PR	Profit = $TR - TE$	$50,000

$$\text{Profit} = \text{Total Revenue} - \text{Total Expense}$$
$$PR = RH \cdot BR - (S + O)$$
$$= 2{,}000 \cdot 200 - (250{,}000 + 100{,}000) = 50{,}000$$

What we are calling profit here is the classical business profit. Remember that Beth requires a salary of $250,000 for herself and considers this a cost of doing business. She wants to ultimately make more than she did in her old job, and this is the reason for the planned profit of $50,000. If her profit is $0, she only breaks even. To find the billing rate at which she breaks even, she sets the profit equal to $0 and solves for the hourly billing rate. We looked at this before, but here we do the math more formally.

$$\text{Profit} = RH \cdot BR - (S + O)$$
$$\$0 = 2{,}000 \cdot (\text{Breakeven } BR) - (\$250{,}000 + \$100{,}000)$$

$$\text{Breakeven } BR = \frac{S+O}{RH} = \frac{350{,}000}{2000} = 175$$

It is clear that Beth wants to make her salary of $250,000 and considers this salary a necessary expense. However Beth is a partner, so her salary is not considered an expense. This means that partner profit is calculated with her overhead as the only expense. We will denote partner profit by *PtPR*.

Partner Profit = Total Revenue – Expense other than partner compensation

$$PtPR = RH \cdot BR - O$$
$$= 2{,}000 \cdot 200 - \$100{,}000 = \$300{,}000$$

Note that the classical profit as a percent of total revenue is 12.5%.

$$\frac{PR}{TR} = \frac{50{,}000}{400{,}000} = 0.125$$

This looks reasonable, but partner profit does not; it is 75% of total revenue.

$$\frac{PtPR}{TR} = \frac{300{,}000}{400{,}000} = 0.75$$

In a large firm things are much more complex and there are salaries (associates, staff) that do count as expenses. The accounting complexity hides the simple math that we see here, not counting essential partner salary as an expense inflates partner profit. Spelling out the math forces us to look at profits with increased precision. To illustrate this further we will return to our example of the effects of discounting and use some mathematical notation for further discussion.

Discounting revisited

Let's think about the effect of a 10% discount on Beth's planned budget for her first year. The next table illustrates what happens if Beth decides to try to gain business by discounting at 10% for the year and reduces her rate per billable hour to 180 from 200.

Variable	Description	Budget	Discount
S	Salary	\$250,000	\$250,000
RH	Realized Hours	2,000	2,000
OO	Direct Overhead	\$100,000	\$100,000
BR	Billing Rate	\$200	\$180
E	Total Expense	\$350,000	\$350,000
TR	Total Revenue = $RH \cdot BR$	\$400,000	\$360,000
PR	Profit = $TR - TE$	\$50,000	\$10,000

By discounting the billable hour rate by 10%, Beth has cut her profit margin from \$50,000 to \$10,000—a reduction of 80%. This should not be a surprise. The 10% discount applied to all revenue of \$400,000, so there was a total discount of \$40,000. The profit of only \$50,000 was reduced by this amount to \$10,000.

We could look at this in a very simple way if we look at profit as a percent of revenue. The planned profit of \$50,000 was 12.5% of revenue. The profit after discount was 2.5% of revenue.

We could have predicted this as follows:

Planned Profit	12.5%	of revenue
– Discount	–10.0%	of revenue
= Actual Profit	2.5%	of revenue

The loss in profit due to discount varies with both discount rate and overhead. Below we give a data table that shows a range of losses in profit based on various combinations of discount rate and overhead in Beth's case.

		Discount Rate			
		5.00%	10.00%	15.00%	20.00%
Overhead	50,000	20.0%	40.0%	60.0%	80.0%
	75,000	26.7%	53.3%	80.0%	106.7%
	100,000	40.0%	80.0%	120.0%	160.0%
	125,000	80.0%	160.0%	240.0%	320.0%

Raising salary would also increase expense, lower profit and make the effect of a discount on profit larger. We can do some "simple" math to sum this up for Beth. We will use the letter d to represent the discount rate. Then we have:

Original planned profit is total revenue less total expense:

$$P_{plan} = TR - E = RH \cdot BR - E$$

Profit after discount changes the billing rate to $BR(1-d)$ so we have:

$$P_{disc} = RH \cdot BR(1-d) - E$$

Then the change in profit is:

$$P_{plan} - P_{disc} = RH \cdot BR - E - \left[RH \cdot BR(1-d) - E \right] = RH \cdot BR \cdot d$$

The percentage change in profit is the change in profit divided by the profit:

$$\frac{RH \cdot BR \cdot d}{RH \cdot BR - E}$$

This formula implies that if Beth keeps her realized hours as planned:

1. Any increase in the discount rate will increase the percentage loss in profit.
2. Any increase in total expense will increase the percentage loss in profit.
3. Beth could offset the effect of the discount (d in the numerator) above by lowering expenses (E) so as to increase the denominator.

But for most lawyers, the main implication is simpler: these relationships are complicated. Before talking to your client about their next discount, you may want to talk to your finance department.

Maintaining profitability

There was a time not very long ago when lawyers did not need to worry about the precise impact of discounting and realization on profits. Everyone knew that discounted rates and low realization were bad because they reduced the total revenue that partners divided up at the end of the year. But nobody got too excited about the details of exactly how bad, nor how to avoid problems. To maintain and increase income, they simply raised their rates.

Those were the days. But then in 2008 the economy declined and clients became more demanding. Associates and staff were laid off, partners felt squeezed, and law firms began to get more serious about protecting profitability.

For a high level overview of law firm profitability, see Toby Brown's excellent series of blog posts, "The Economics of Law and the Future of Legal Knowledge Management."[199] His five-part series explains the four key drivers of law firm profits: rates, realization, productivity, and leverage. Realization was addressed in Chapter 2, and productivity and leverage are beyond the scope of this book. But before we proceed to a discussion of law firm pricing actions, this section will take one last look at tactics to maintain profitability in challenging times.

Consider the example of a matter which is supposed to bring in $30,000 in billable hour revenue. The allocation of that $30,000 in revenue to salary, overhead and partner profit/compensation will vary from firm to firm, and even from one matter to another. But as a simple starting point, assume that one-third goes to each, like this:

Total revenue	$30,000
Salary	$10,000
Overhead	$10,000
Partner Profit	$10,000

Now suppose that the client demands a 10% discount and gets it. Then $3,000 of total revenue is lost. Since salary and overhead must be paid, the $3,000 loss must come out of partner profit/compensation. The result looks like this:

Total revenue	$27,000
Salary	$10,000
Overhead	$10,000
Partner Profit	$ 7,000

In this example, the drop in partner profit is 30%, not 10%. There is a multiplier effect in which the 10% loss in revenue is multiplied by three.

This multiplier effect will occur with any 10% loss in revenue, whatever the source. If it is due to a refusal to pay the full bill or a write-off, the effect is the same: Planned partner profits drop by $3,000 or 30%. Anything that keeps you from getting your full, planned billing rate has a much larger impact on profit than you might think. Because you are tempted to say, "It is only a 10% reduction," the full impact of the loss on profits may be underestimated.

The multiplier will vary depending on the financial specifics of each case: it could easily be higher or lower than three. But whatever the financial structure of the firm, there is a material multiplier affecting profits, and it is hidden from those who do not get the math.

As times have gotten tougher in the last few years, the first step many firms took was to lower their costs by reducing salary and overhead expenses. This helps, but not as much as reduced discounting or increased realization would.

Consider the effects of a 10% cost reduction on this matter. If we kept revenue the same, but cut both salary and overhead by 10%, the result would look like this:

Total revenue	$30,000
Salary	$ 9,000
Overhead	$ 9,000
Partner Profit	$12,000

Saving 10% in cost saves $2,000 and thus can add 20% to partner profit. However, as we saw above, losing 10% of income to discounting or realization took 30% out of partner profit.

Thus a 10% reduction in cost has less effect than a 10% loss in revenue. The reason is simple enough: a 10% loss in revenue is applied to all of revenue, but the 10% reduction in cost acts only on the two-thirds of revenue that is applied to costs.

Again, the core lesson for most lawyers is simple: Before you try to improve firm profitability by implementing changes in spending, you would be wise to get a second opinion from a financial professional. In fact, these things are often subject to assumptions and interpretations, so a third opinion and a fourth may be in order too.

Endnotes

[1] Copyright 2011 and 2012 Bloomberg Finance L.P. Originally published by Bloomberg Finance L.P. Reprinted with permission. The opinions expressed are those of the authors.

[2] Reprinted with permission from Legal Management magazine, Volume 31 Issue 7, published by the Association of Legal Administrators, www.alanet.org.

[3] http://www.altmanweil.com/dir_docs/resource/ad3048ed-a438-4fd0-8c96-1597498c841f_document.pdf

[4] http://adverselling.typepad.com/how_law_firms_sell/2005/06/an_11_million_f.html

[5] http://www.abajournal.com/news/article/facing_the_alternative/

[6] Speaking Different Languages: Alternative Fee Arrangements (AFAs) for Law Firms and Legal Departments, http://almlegalintel.com/Surveys/AFAreport

[7] Brian Baxter, "Demise of Dewey Eclipses Deaths of Smaller Firms, "*The Am Law Daily* (September 9, 2012).

[8] Julie Triedman, Sara Randazzo, and Brian Baxter, "House of Cards, "*The American Lawyer* (July 2012), 49.

[9] http://www.adamsmithesq.com/2012/09/growth-is-dead-part-i/

[10] Robert Herbold, *Seduced by Success* (McGraw Hill, 2007), 5.

[11] For a much longer list of business failures, see: http://en.wikipedia.org/wiki/List_of_business_failures

[12] Richard Susskind, *Tomorrow's Lawyers* (Oxford University Press, 2013), 3.

[13] http://www.altmanweil.com/dir_docs/resource/1667e5c8-b99e-4557-93ac-73174118ea29_document.pdf

[14] The question about efficiency was added after 2009, so it was not possible to compare results for the two years.

[15] Stephen J. Poor, "Re-Engineering the Business of Law," DealBook blog/*New York Times* (May 7, 2012), http://dealbook.nytimes.com/2012/05/07/re-engineering-the-business-of-law/

[16] Jim Hassett, *The LegalBizDev Guide to Alternative Fees*, (Boston: LegalBizDev, 2009), 142.

[17] ALM Legal Intelligence, "Legal Project Management: Much Promise, Many Hurdles," August 2012.

[18] The remainder was almost equally split between "no" (26%), and "not sure" (22%). The people who chose to answer this survey had opted in to an LPM survey, so the fact that they are not sure what their own firm is doing says a great deal about the pioneering status of this area.

[19] Jim Hassett, "Teaching Lawyers How to Manage: Can It Improve the Bottom Line," *The Am Law Daily* (March 18, 2010), http://amlawdaily.typepad.com/amlawdaily/2010/03/hassett.html.

[20] Gina Passarella, "Dechert Puts Its Attorneys Through Project Management Training," *Legal Intelligencer*, (April 2, 2010), http://www.law.com/jsp/article.jsp?id=1202447368069&Dechert_Puts_Its_Attorneys_Through_Project_Management_Training&slreturn=20120826221238.

[21] http://www.almlegalintel.com/SurveyDescription.aspx?id=xSm7KzduNUc=&type=fEFglaD+grg=, 17.

[22] http://adverselling.typepad.com/how_law_firms_sell/2012/02/index.html

[23] For an example of realization calculations, consider a small matter that required 10 hours of partner time at $400 ($4,000) and 40 hours of associate time at $200 ($8,000) for a total of $12,000. But the relationship partner feels that the associate could have been much more efficient and decides to bill only 20 of the 40 associate hours and write off the rest. He sends out a bill for $8,000 ($4,000 for 10 partner hours at $400 plus another $4,000 for 20 associate hours at $200). When billing realization is calculated based on the actual rates charged to this client, the rate is 66.7% (the $8,000 actually billed divided by the $12,000 value of the time cost at discounted rates). However,

some firms calculate billing realization based not on actual hourly rates for a particular client, but rather on the standard rates for each lawyer before discounts. Assume that this particular client had negotiated a 20% discount, and that the partner's standard rate is $500 and the associate's standard rate is $250. In that case, the value of the original time is $15,000 ($5,000 for 10 partner hours at $500 plus $10,000 for 40 associate hours at $250), and the billing realization rate is just 53.3% (the $8,000 actually billed divided by the $15,000 value of the time at standard rates). This rate reflects both the discount and the write-off. Now suppose the client feels that the $8,000 bill was too high, argues his case, and ends up paying only $7,000. This yields a collection realization rate of 87.5% (the $7,000 paid divided by the $8,000 billed). In this example, if it were based on actual discounted rates, total realization would be 58.3% ($7,000 paid divided by the $12,000 value of the time at discounted rates.) If it were based on standard rates, it would go down to 46.7% ($7,000 paid divided by the $15,000 value of the time at standard rates).

[24] According to the 2007 Law Firm Economic Survey by Lexis Nexis, "Billing realization has a relationship to increased partner income while collection realization doesn't." (To our knowledge, this is the latest available data.) In other words, lawyers are paid for billing more hours, whether clients pay for them or not. From a straight business point of view, this is a bad idea. You get what you pay for. So when firms pay lawyers for billing more hours, whether clients actually pay those bills or not, they create a culture that values billing more than getting paid. The results of this can be seen in the data on realization rates at large firms, which are not pretty.

[25] Hildebrandt Institute and Citi Private Bank, *2012 Client Advisory,* 2.

[26] http://newsandinsight.thomsonreuters.com/uploadedFiles/Reuters_Content/2012/07_-_July/PMI_Q2_2012_v1.0-2.pdf

[27] ALM Legal Intelligence, "Legal Project Management: Much Promise, Many Hurdles," 8.

[28] http://www.legalprojectmanagement.info/blog/

[29] Barbara Boake and Rick Kathuria, *Project Management for Lawyers* (London: Ark Group, 2011), 14.

[30] http://gimbalcanada.com/blog/2012/10/2/oh-we-already-do-thatwe-have-legal-project-management-why-pr.html

[31] ALM Legal Intelligence, "Legal Project Management: Much Promise, Many Hurdles."

[32] When the ALM survey asked, "At any time did you turn to outside help or consultants to help formulate a project management initiative?" 55% said yes, which translate to 59 out of 108 respondents. These 59 were asked about the type of consultant, and 6% chose the Seyfarth option quoted above. That translates to four people, although we do not know whether they represented four different forms, or whether any came from Seyfarth itself.

[33] Personal communication.

[34] Laura Colcord and Catherine Alman MacDonagh, "Legal Lean Sigma™: Process improvement for the legal industry," (presentation through *West LegalEdcenter*, May 2010).

[35] http://www.knowledge-management-online.com/Definition-of-Knowledge-Management.html#VisitorPages

[36] http://read.uberflip.com/i/68817/4

[37] www.pmi.org

[38] Kevin Marron, "Buzzword 2010: project management," *Canadian Lawyer* (April 2010), http://www.canadianlawyermag.com/Buzzword-2010-project-management.html

[39] http://www.geeklawblog.com/2011/06/elephant-post-is-it-legal-project.html

[40] David Maister, "Are Law Firms Manageable?" *The American Lawyer* (April 2006).

[41] Stacy D. Ballin and Mitchell S. Thompson, "Why We Decided to Become Certified Legal Project Managers," *National Law Review* (4 Feb. 2011), http://www.natlawreview.com/article/why-we-decided-to-become-certified-legal-project-managers.

[42] http://www.acc.com/education/businessedu/programs/projectmgmt.cfm

[43] http://www.lexpertdigital.ca/lexpert/201105?pg=48#

[44] Ibid.

[45] ALM Legal Intelligence, "Legal Project Management: Much Promise, Many Hurdles,"19.

[46] ALM Legal Intelligence, "Legal Project Management: Much Promise, Many Hurdles," 15.

[47] http://adverselling.typepad.com/how_law_firms_sell/2011/06/four-ways-lawyers-should-improve-project-management.html

[48] Richard Susskind, *The End of Lawyers?* (USA: Oxford University Press, 2010), 280.

[49] http://amlawdaily.typepad.com/amlawdaily/2010/03/hassett.html

[50] All right. We admit it. We haven't been thrilled when we've seen some competitors reproduce the list word for word as if it were their own.

[51] Erik Verzuh, *The Fast Forward MBA in Project Management* (Hoboken: Wiley Publishing, 1999), 134.

[52] www.utbms.com. The nature of the UTBMS system, and the way it is being used, is continuing to evolve to this day, as discussed in the third edition of our *Legal Project Management Quick Reference Guide*.

[53] Copies of this form and the others used in coaching can be found in the *Legal Project Management Quick Reference Guide*.

[54] http://amlawdaily.typepad.com/amlawdaily/2010/03/0319future.html

[55] http://www.prismlegal.com/wordpress/index.php?p=1026&c=1

[56] The "80/20 rule" has been attributed to the nineteenth century Italian economist Vifredo Pareto, and there are many variations, including "Eighty percent of your business comes from 20 percent of your customers," "Eighty percent of the work is done by 20 percent of the people" and "Eighty percent of all beer is consumed by 20 percent of beer drinkers."

[57] Quoted in Jerome Agel and Walter D. Glanze, *Pearls of Wisdom: A Harvest of Quotations from All Ages* (William Morrow Paperbacks, 1987), 46.

[58] http://en.wikipedia.org/wiki/Space_Pen

[59] http://www.snopes.com/business/genius/spacepen.asp

[60] http://www.summitlaw.com/PalumboArticle.pdf

[61] Personal communication, December 2012

[62] http://newsandinsight.thomsonreuters.com/uploadedFiles/Reuters_Content/2012/07_-_July/PMI_Q2_2012_v1.0-2.pdf

[63] http://www.patrickmckenna.com/PatrickJMcKennaBrainmatterCreationsHeardingCats40029.aspx

[64] ALM Legal Intelligence, "Legal Project Management: Much Promise, Many Hurdles," 14.

[65] Full disclosure: Some of the firms in Chapter 4, and all of the firms in Chapter 5 are LegalBizDev clients who have used our behavior change programs. In Chapter 4, however, the discussion will be limited to non-LegalBizDev approaches.

[66] Carla Goldstein and Lisa Damon, "Case study 2: Seyfarth Shaw LLP—Lean in action," in *The Legal Process Improvement Toolkit*, by Chris Bull (USA: Ark Group, 2012), 103.

[67] Goldstein and Damon, "Case study 2," 102.

[68] Craig Gig, Neil Decal, and Stephen R. Covey, *Six Sigma for Dummies* (Hoboken: Wiley Publishing, 2005), 10.

[69] ABA Journal, "New Buzz Phrase in Efficiency Efforts," www.abajournal.com/news/article/new_buzz_phrase_in_efficiency_efforts_process_management

[70] Toyota's seven wastes were excess inventory, excess processing, overproduction, transportation, motion, waiting, and defects. For details, see en.wikipedia.org/wiki/Lean_manufacturing and en.wikipedia.org/wiki/Toyota_Production_System

[71] Personal communication, Kim Craig, December 14, 2012. Kim is the Director of Seyfarth's Legal Project Management Office, which has a staff of 18 professional project managers.

[72] http://www.dailyreportonline.com/PubArticleDRO.jsp ?id=1202566995546&thepage=4

[73] D.M. Levine, "Leap of Faith," *The American Lawyer*, April 1, 2010.

[74] Goldstein and Damon, "Case study 2," 103-104.

[75] Passarella, "Dechert."

[76] Alan Cohen, "How Six Big Law Firms Get Serious About Project Management," *Law Technology News*, August 13, 2012.

[77] Barbara Boake and Rick Kathuria, *Project Management for Lawyers* (Ark Group, 2011), 80.

[78] Cohen, "Six Big Law Firms."

[79] Boake and Kathuria, *Project Management*, 82.

[80] Boake and Kathuria, *Project Management*, 79.

[81] Cohen, "Six Big Law Firms."

[82] Cohen, "Six Big Law Firms."

[83] http://adverselling.typepad.com/how_law_firms_sell/2012/06/tracking-legal-costs-with-task-codes-different-firms-take-different-approaches-part-3-of-3.html

[84] ALM Legal Intelligence, "Legal Project Management: Much Promise, Many Hurdles," 17.

[85] ALM Legal Intelligence, "Legal Project Management: Much Promise, Many Hurdles," 16.

[86] Susan Hackett, Barb Dawson and Laura Ariane Miller, "Valuing Litigation: Lessons Learned from Collaboration," *ACC Docket* (May 2011), 130.

[87] Jim Hassett, *The LegalBizDev Guide to Alternative Fees*, (Boston: LegalBizDev, 2009), 142.

[88] www.sciencedirect.com/science?_ob=ArticleURL&_udi B6V9V433PBK53&_user=10&_coverDate=07%2F31%2F2001&_alid=1314695237&_rdoc=1&_fmt=high&_orig=search&_cdi=5908&_sort=r&_docanchor=&view=c&_ct=631&_acct=C000050221&_version=1&_urlVersion=0&_userid=10&md5=d0e6cedc277e256b18529002fc232edb

[89] http://amlawdaily.typepad.com/amlawdaily/2010/03/hassett.html

[90] http://www.law.com/jsp/article.jsp?id=1202447368069 &Dechert_Puts_Its_Attorneys_Through_Project_Management_Training&slreturn=20120806081352

[91] Personal correspondence, June 2010.

[92] This is an intensive program, designed for the very small number of lawyers and staff who are willing and able to devote significant time to studying the most influential texts in the field, and analyzing how to adapt these best practices to the unique challenges and culture of their firm. The majority of the people who have participated to date were already leading their group's LPM efforts when they signed up and came to our program looking for more.

[93] Paul Lippe, "Emerging trends that are changing how lawyers and law firms work," in *The Future of Legal Services*, 30.

[94] http://www.inhouseaccess.com/2010/10/01/a-value-based-client-firm-relationship-part-xvi/

[95] http://dealbook.nytimes.com/2012/05/07/re-engineering-the-business-of-law/

[96] http://www.inhouseaccess.com/2011/02/10/a-value-based-client-firm-relationship-part-iii-2/

[97] Jim Hassett, *The LegalBizDev Survey of Alternative Fees* (LegalBizDev, 2009), http://www.legalbizdev.com/alternativefees/survey.html

[98] http://www.adamsmithesq.com/2012/09/growth-is-dead-part-i/

[99] http://www.altmanweil.com/dir_docs/resource/88adb851-ba55-4cce-9d97-fa06607c75bb_document.pdf

[100] Thomas T. Nagle, John E. Hogan and Joseph Zale, *The Strategy and Tactics of Pricing: A Guide to Growing More Profitably, Fifth Edition* (Prentice Hall, 2010), 98.

[101] Claire Zillman, "Expense Report," *The American Lawyer* (May 30, 2012), 67.

[102] "The AM Law 100: Firms Ranked by Profits Per Partner," *The American Lawyer* (May 1, 2012).

[103] Ronald J. Baker, *Pricing on Purpose: Creating and Capturing* Value (Wiley, 2006), 88.

[104] Nagle, Hogan and Hale, *Strategy*, 2-3.

[105] Hassett, *Survey*, 43.

[106] Association of Corporate Counsel, *ACC Value-Based Fee Primer*, (Washington DC: Association of Corporate Counsel, July 2010), 31.

[107] http://www.abajournal.com/news/article/law_firm_price _wars_break_out_as_some_try_loss_leader_bids_for_work

[108] http://adverselling.typepad.com/how_law_firms_sell/2009/ 11/price-wars.html

[109] http://www.americanlawyer.com/PubArticleTAL.jsp ?id=1202572358253&thepage=1

[110] 21% fired their law firms because they were too expensive, 18% for "bad advice or no expertise," and 15% for poor service.

[111] http://www.americanlawyer.com/PubArticleTAL.jsp?id=1202579458620

[112] http://www.altmanweil.com/LFiT2011/

[113] ALM Legal Intelligence, *Speaking Different Languages: Alternative Fee Arrangements for Law Firms and Legal Departments* (April 2012), http://www.lexisnexis.com/counsellink/documents/ALM-Survey-Alternative-Fee-Arrangements.pdf

[114] Nagle, Hogan and Hale, *Strategy*, 4.

[115] Ron Paquette, "Cracking the Acorn Theory," *Strategies: The Journal of Legal Marketing* (Sep 2007).

[116] Paquette, "Acorn Theory."

[117] Ronald J. Baker, *Implementing Value Pricing: A Radical Business Model for Professional Firms* (Wiley, 2010), 233.

[118] Baker, *Implementing*, 22.

[119] Baker, *Implementing,* 160.

[120] James A. Durham, *The Essential Little Book of Great Lawyering* (James A. Durham, 2006).

[121] Jim Hassett, *Legal Business Development Quick Reference Guide, Second Edition* (LegalBizDev, 2012).

[122] Baker, *Implementing*, 289.

[123] Baker, *Implementing*, 241.

[124] Baker, *Implementing*, 245-257.

[125] Baker, *Implementing*, 275.

[126] http://www.verasage.com/index.php/community/how_to _value_price_just_do_it/

[127] Nagle, Hogan, and Zale, *Strategy*, 19.

[128] Nagle, Hogan, and Zale, *Strategy*, 72.

[129] Nagle, Hogan, and Zale, *Strategy*, 75.

[130] Nagle, Hogan, and Zale, *Strategy*, 117.

[131] Nagle, Hogan, and Zale, *Strategy*, 105.

[132] Nagle, Hogan, and Zale, *Strategy*, 107.

[133] Nagle, Hogan, and Zale, *Strategy*, 108.

[134] http://www.bartlit-beck.com/about-success.html

[135] http://adverselling.typepad.com/how_law_firms_sell/2009/ 04/the-law-firm-of-the-future-is-open-for-business.html

[136] Matt Laws later became Director of Client Services & Pricing at Crowell & Moring

[137] http://www.acc.com/valuechallenge/valueindex/index_old2.cfm

[138] http://www.lawweekonline.com/2011/11/acc-value-index-ending/

[139] http://www.integreon.com/blog/2011/03/value-how-do-we-define-it-how-do-we-measure-it-live-from-georgetown-law.html

[140] http://www.abajournal.com/legalrebels/article/what_if _someone_could_measure_what_lawyers_do/

[141] http://www.inhouseaccess.com/2010/06/17/a-value-based-client-firm-relationship

[142] http://www.inhouseaccess.com/2010/07/08/a-value-based-client-firm-relationship-part-iv/

[143] http://www.inhouseaccess.com/2010/07/08/a-value-based-client-firm-relationship-part-iv/

[144] http://www.inhouseaccess.com/2010/07/27/a-value-based-client-firm-relationship-part-vi/

[145] http://www.inhouseaccess.com/2010/09/articles/clientfirm-value/a-valuebased-clientfirm-relationship-part-xiii/

[146] http://adverselling.typepad.com/how_law_firms_sell/2012/ 01/legal-pricing-part-4-value-pricing-basics-.html

[147] http://www.geeklawblog.com/2012/01/staying-relevant-part-1-perfect-storm.html

[148] http://www.abajournal.com/legalrebels/article/what_if_someone_could_measure_what_lawyers_do/

[149] Hassett, *Survey*, 47.

[150] Hassett, *Survey*, 48.

[151] http://www.geeklawblog.com/2012/01/staying-relevant-part-1-perfect-storm.html

[152] Hildebrandt, *Client Advisory,* 10.

[153] http://www.abajournal.com/legalrebels/article/lawyer_comp_the_third_rail_of_legal_value_conversations/

[154] Hildebrandt, *Client Advisory*, 5.

[155] http://intelligentchallenge.com/2011/10/28/excuse-me-i-think-your-pricing-is-broken/

[156] American Bar Association, *ABA Commission on Billable Hours Report, 2001-2002* (2002).

[157] ABA Report, 5.

[158] ABA Report, 8.

[159] http://www.amazon.com/Winning-Alternatives-Billable-Hour-2nd/dp/1590311175/ref=sr_1_4?ie=UTF8&s=books&qid=1230316424&sr=1-4

[160] ABA Report, 8.

[161] In 1999, the US Small Business Administration named us the best government contractor in New England.

[162] http://www.verasage.com/index.php/community/what_a_great_idea/

[163] Patrick Lamb, *Alternative Fee Arrangements: Value Fees and the Changing Legal Market* (Ark Group, 2010), 31.

[164] http://www.americanlawyer.com/PubArticleTAL.jsp?id=1202579458620

[165] *Speaking Different Languages*

[166] ABA Report, ix.

[167] http://www.dupontlegalmodel.com/onlinelibrary_detail.asp?libid=96

[168] http://www.nytimes.com/2009/01/30/business/30hours.html?_r=3&pagewanted=2&partner=permalink&exprod=permalink

[169] http://adverselling.typepad.com/how_law_firms_sell/2009/06/alternative-fees-part-16-winwin-or-winlose.html#comments

[170] Thomas S. Clay and Eric A. Seeger, *2012 Law Firms in Transition*, (Newtown Square: Altman Weil, 2012), iv.

[171] Hassett, *Survey*.

[172] http://www.bizjournals.com/columbus/stories/2010/06/21/tidbits4.html

[173] http://www.acc.com/legalresources/resource.cfm?show=1294806

[174] Note that ACC asked about the "percent of work" which may give a different answer than the "percent of revenue" surveys discussed elsewhere in this book. If nine out of 10 matters are hourly, that could be considered 90% of all work, even if the one non-hourly matter cost more than the other nine combined.

[175] *Speaking Different Languages*

[176] A "flat fee with shared savings" is a kind of risk collar, in which there is no shared risk for going over budget, "If at the conclusion of the work fees calculated on the basis of the hours worked would be less than the flat fee, the client and the law firm share the savings."

[177] http://www.dupontlegalmodel.com/onlinelibrary_detail.asp?libid=96

[178] Association of Corporate Counsel, *2011 Chief Legal Officer Survey* (2011).

[179] http://www.summitlaw.com/PalumboArticle.pdf

[180] http://finance.yahoo.com/news/For-Large-Firms-Alternative-law-15342292.html?.v=1

[181] http://www.dupontlegalmodel.com/alternative-fees-for-litigation-improved-control-and-higher-value/

[182] Mark Wolf and Kerry Notestine, "Controlling outside counsel costs through an alternative billing model," *ACC Docket*, May 2008, 70-84.

[183] Hassett, *Survey*.

[184] http://www.valoremlaw.com/what/value-line-adjustment.html

[185] http://www.summitlaw.com/PalumboArticle.pdf

[186] http://amlawdaily.typepad.com/amlawdaily/2009/06/success-of-alternative-fees-depends-on-trust.html

[187] http://amlawdaily.typepad.com/amlawdaily/2009/06/success-of-alternative-fees-depends-on-trust.html

[188] Christopher Meyer and Julia Kirby, "The Big Idea: Leadership in the Age of Transparency," *Harvard Business Review* (April 2010), http://hbr.org/2010/04/the-big-idea-leadership-in-the-age-of-transparency/ar/1

[189] *Speaking Different Languages*

[190] Susan Hackett, "Six Critical Strategies Used By Law Firm Pricing Directors," *Corporate Counsel*, (September 27, 2012), http://www.law.com/corporatecounsel/PubArticleCC.jsp?id=1202572601682&6_Critical_Strategies_Used_By_Law_Firm_Pricing_Directors&slreturn=20120909060900

[191] http://www.acc.com/legalresources/resource.cfm?show=1308701

[192] http://www.acc.com/legalresources/resource.cfm?show=1308701, Figure 2.

[193] http://www.jdsupra.com/legalnews/the-2012-edge-international-global-partn-82238/

[194] http://www.jdsupra.com/legalnews/the-2012-edge-international-global-partn-82238/

[195] http://www.jdsupra.com/legalnews/the-2012-edge-international-global-partn-82238/

[196] http://www.altmanweil.com/LFiT2012/

[197] *Speaking Different Languages*

[198] http://www.jdsupra.com/legalnews/the-2012-edge-international-global-partn-82238/

[199] http://www.geeklawblog.com/2012/10/the-economics-of-law-and-future-of.html

Index

A

ABA Commission on Billable Hours Report, 143, 145
ACC Value Challenge, 16, 74, 112, 130, 183
Acritas, 109
Adams and Reese, 186, 187, 191
Adams, Chuck, 186, 191
Agile, 69
Akin Gump, 69, 125, 129, 136, 215
ALM Legal Intelligence Survey, 13, 15, 21, 24, 32, 48, 64, 110, 148, 149, 156, 162, 163, 165, 185, 192, 215
Altman Weil, 9, 95, 96, 109, 137, 148, 149, 154, 155, 156, 214
American Bar Association, 40, 58, 143
AmLaw 100, 23
Association of Corporate Counsel, 16, 32, 40, 64, 72, 76, 80, 108, 129, 130, 131, 146, 157, 166, 183
Axelrod, Alan, 91

B

Baker & McKenzie, 58–59, 124, 128, 136
Baker, Ron, 98, 103, 112–19, 133, 146
Ballin, Stacy, 31, 72
Barnett, Ben, 52
Bartlit Beck Herman Palenchar & Scott, 124, 179
Bartlit, Fred, 124, 179, 180
Bell, Steve, 181
Best practices, 27, 33, 44, 83–88, 129, 166
Bidding process, 128
Bilzin Sumberg, 66, 87–93

Binder, Carl, 24
Boake, Barbara, 22, 52
Bohr, Niels, 10
Borden, Bennett, 33
Brandt, Jeff, 29
Brown, Toby, 69, 125, 129, 137, 138, 215
Budget, 13, 17, 20, 26, 27, 31, 34, 37–43, 44, 47–60, 67, 72, 73, 82, 85, 87, 88, 90, 91, 97, 106, 108, 110, 118, 126, 127, 128, 131, 151, 161, 162, 167, 170, 181, 189, 197–200, 205, 219
Burke, Steve, 79, 80, 81
Butler Snow, 190
Byrd, Michael, 125, 126, 127

C

Cain, Kathrine, 126
Carr, Jeff, 172
Carve-outs, 91
Certified Legal Project Manager® program, 32, 33, 66, 74
Change orders, 39, 117, 169, 170, 199
Chassen, Jon, 87, 88
Christensen, Bruce Clearing Sky, 97
Citi Private Bank, 139
Client Advisory, 139, 140
Client satisfaction, 54, 58, 76, 110, 125, 126, 129, 153, 181, 205, 206
Coaching, 2, 22, 26, 31, 38, 40, 41, 65, 66, 70, 74, 87–93
Cohen, Alan, 51
Commercial litigation, 50
Conservative risk avoidance, 177–80
Contingencies, 88, 90, 124, 157, 160, 171–73, 174, 179, 187, 188, 196, 199, 214
Contingent fees, 171–73, 187, 188, 196, 199
Cooper, Jonathan, 33, 59, 188, 189
Cordo, Vince, 72
Cost-plus pricing, 98, 99–105, 112, 113, 122, 144
Courson, Gardner, 150, 168, 172
Cragwall, Jr., J.A., 189
Critical Path Method, 28
Crowell & Moring, 187–88

D

Damon, Lisa, 51, 63, 131
Data mining, 108
Dechert, 14, 48, 52–54, 63, 68
Dewey & LeBoeuf, 7
Discounting, 110, 120, 165, 218, 219–21

Dodds, Stuart, 59, 124, 125
Domson, Allison, 81
Dotson, Al, 87, 88
Duane Morris, 171
Due diligence, 56, 91, 190
DuPont, 28, 49, 179, 180, 185
Durham, Jim, 114, 138

E

Easton, Paul, 21
Edge International, 152
Eight key issues in legal project management, 20, 38, 39, 41, 42, 75, 198
Eighty/twenty rule, 44
End of Lawyers?, The, 37
Ende, Chris, 215
Engagement letter, 17, 27, 38, 72, 83
Essential Little Book of Great Lawyering, The, 114

F

Farris, Vaughan, Wills & Murphy, 32
Fasken Martineau, 60
Fast Forward MBA in Project Management, The, 40
Feagin, Bob, 17
Fee cap, 128, 158, 161, 187
Fenwick & West, 57–58
Fields, Rob, 180, 181
Fish & Richardson, 127
Fixed fee, 17, 80, 81, 91, 106, 108, 123, 127, 135, 141, 150, 151, 153, 157, 158, 159, 171, 178, 179, 181, 183, 186, 190, 192, 193, 197, 199
FMC Technologies, 172
Foley & Lardner, 60–62
Friedmann, Ron, 44
Furlong, Jordan, 152

G

Gavin, Keri, 126
Georgetown Law School, 130
Glitzenstein, Kurt, 127
Global Partner Compensation Survey, 211
Goldblatt, Samuel, 54, 55
Goldstein, Carla, 49–51
Goodwin Proctor, 215
Grady, Ken, 76, 131, 132
Grauer, Dave, 75
Gray Plant Mooty, 66, 81–86

H

Hackett, Susan, 130, 139, 205
Hannigan, Jim, 58
Hartmann, Markus, 209, 211, 212, 215
Heller Ehrman, 7

Herman, Skip, 124
Hogan, John, 97, 119
Holdback, 160
Holland & Knight, 17
Howrey, 7

I

Inside counsel, 200, 201
International Legal Technology Association, 27, 129

J

Jarrett-Kerr, Nick, 211
Johnson III, Charles, 190
Just-in-time training, 65, 66, 67, 68, 70, 77–86

K

K&L Gates, 185, 187, 190
Kalis, Peter, 185, 190, 191
Kalogerou, Byron, 56, 57
Kathuria, Rick, 22, 52
Kirmayer, Kathy, 187, 188
Knowledge management, 22, 26, 27, 222

L

Lamb, Patrick, 162, 179
Langevin, Judy, 84–86
Law Firms in Transition Survey, 9, 95, 148, 156, 214
Laws, Matt, 125, 128
Legal OnRamp, 14, 74, 180
Legal project management, 27
LegalBizDev Guide to Alternative Fees, 181
LegalBizDev Survey of Alternative Fees, 95, 105, 107, 109, 138, 141, 147, 153, 155, 157
Lessons learned review, 54, 75, 131, 171
Lippe, Paul, 14, 42, 74, 130, 137
Litigation investment model, 209–16
Littler Mendelson, 173

M

MacEwen, Bruce, 8, 95
Mais, Joseph, 186, 191, 192
Maister, David, 30
Marriott International, 165
Matter Planning Template, 40
Mayer Brown, 126, 127, 136
McCarthy Tétrault, 32
McDermott Will & Emery, 56–57
McKelvey, Stewart, 32
McKenna, Patrick, 47
Metrics, 129–37
Mitchell, Keith, 32
Mordan, Bill, 209, 211, 212, 215
Morford, Joe, 156

Morgan Lewis, 25, 154
Morley, Sean, 60
Morris James, 64
Morrison & Foerster, 16, 150
Mortgage services, 25

N

Nagle, Thomas, 97, 119
NASA, 45
Negotiate change orders, 20, 39
Nehema Auerbach, Nicole, 80
New normal, 8, 42, 43
Nihill, Colleen, 52, 53
Nixon Peabody, 10, 54–55, 63, 66
Norton Rose Group, 32

O

O'Brien, Shelbie, 82, 83
Ogilvy Renault, 32
Osler, 32

P

Palumbo, Ralph, 46, 169, 174, 175
Paquette, Ron, 111
Paragon Risk Management Services, 17
Paris, John, 78
Perkins Coie, 186, 187, 191
PERT, 28
Poor, Steve, 9, 49, 77, 156
Pricing on Purpose, 103
Prime, Sarah, 58
Process improvement, 22, 23–26, 31, 51, 59, 133, 138, 156
Project Management Body of Knowledge, The, 22
Project Management for Lawyers, 22, 52
Project Management Institute, 21, 22, 29

R

Realization, 15–20, 46, 58, 74, 150, 205, 214, 221–23
Reduce costs, 45, 49
Reed Smith, 125, 128
Retainer, 157, 159
Reynolds, Karen, 82, 83, 84
Risk, 15, 16, 20, 21, 37, 39, 41, 44, 59, 61, 73, 80, 90, 106, 117, 130, 135, 138, 139, 140, 144, 145, 152, 167, 168, 171, 173, 177–82, 189, 203, 215
Risk analysis, 41
Risk Analysis Template, 41
Risk collar, 161, 162, 188, 189
Risk management, 16, 17
Riskin, Gerry, 48
Rosenblatt, Richard, 154
Roster, Mike, 16, 183

S

Sager, Tom, 49
Scope, 17, 20, 38–42, 55, 79–81, 117, 169, 171, 175, 198, 199
Seyfarth Shaw, 9, 23, 24, 48–51, 63, 76, 77, 131, 132, 133, 156
Seyfarth*Lean*, 48–51, 156
Shadow billing, 182–84
Shindell, Jim, 92, 93
Shomper, James, 150, 168, 172
Shook Hardy & Bacon, 6
Shumate, Keith, 75
Simon, David, 61
Six Sigma, 31, 48–52, 156
Smith, Mark, 140
Spizzirri, Christopher, 64
Squire Sanders, 31, 66, 72–77
Statement of work, 38, 85
Strategy and Tactics of Pricing, The, 97, 110, 119–22
Stutz, Heather, 75
Summit Law Group, 46, 169, 174
Sump, David, 144
Susskind, Richard, 9, 37

T

Tasks, 20, 39, 40, 44, 53, 56, 58, 60, 82, 85, 90, 92, 124, 129, 134, 135, 139, 190, 196, 197
Team, 27
Thacher Profitt & Wood, 7
Thelen Reid & Priest, 7
Thompson, Mitch, 31
Thomson Reuters, 18, 46, 53
Three Geeks and a Law Blog, 29
Time management, 22
Tomorrow's Lawyers, 9
Tradeoffs, 64
Transparency, 59, 149, 182, 184, 215
Troutman & Sanders, 144
Trueheart, Harry, 10, 66
Tucker Ellis, 33, 59, 156, 188, 189
Turner, Bill, 129
Tyco, 6

U

UTBMS, 40

V

Valorem, 80, 162, 174, 179
Value adjustment line, 174–75
Value pricing, 98, 103, 112–19, 119, 133, 136
Value-Based Fee Primer, 108
Verzuh, Erik, 40

W

Wachtell, Lipton, Rosen & Katz, 102
Wagner, Scott, 89, 90
Warner Norcross & Judd, 97, 189
Webb, Camden, 35, 78, 79, 81, 206
Wesemann, Ed, 211
Westlaw, 180
Widom, Mitch, 87, 88
Williams Mullen, 33, 66, 77–81, 206
Williams, Paul, 6
Williamson, Mark, 81, 82, 83
Wilson, Kirsty, 59
Winston & Strawn, 126
Wolverine Worldwide, 76, 131
Womble Carlyle, 128, 180, 181
Work breakdown structure, 40, 85

Z

Zale, Joseph, 97, 119

About the author

Jim Hassett is the founder of LegalBizDev, which helps law firms increase client satisfaction and profitability by improving project management, business development, and alternative fees. Before he started working with lawyers, Jim had 20 years of experience as a sales trainer and consultant to companies from American Express to Zurich Financial Services. He is the author of 11 books, including *The Legal Project Management Quick Reference Guide*, *The LegalBizDev Survey of Alternative Fees,* and *The Legal Business Development Quick Reference Guide*. He has also published more than 80 articles in the *New York Times Magazine*, *Bloomberg Law, Managing Partner, Legal Management, Strategies: The Journal of Legal Marketing, Of Counsel,* and other publications. Jim is a frequent speaker at law firms and at bar associations (including the New York City Bar, the New York State Bar, and the Massachusetts Bar), Harvard Law School, the Association of Corporate Counsel, the Defense Research Institute, the Ark Group, and at Legal Marketing Association meetings in Boston, New York, Philadelphia,

Washington, Savannah, and Vancouver. He has conducted webinars through West LegalEdcenter, the National Law Journal, The International Lawyers Network, TAG Academy, and the Legal Marketing Association. Jim writes the blog *Legal Business Development* which was featured at the ABA TECHSHOW in 2009 and again in 2010 (in its list of "60 Sites: Latest and Greatest Internet Hits") and by TechnoLawyer (in its list of "the most influential legal blogs" in BlawgWorld). He earned his Ph.D. in psychology from Harvard University.

LegalBizDev helps law firms increase client satisfaction and profitability by improving project management, pricing, and business development. We offer coaching, webinars, workshops, retreats, train the trainer programs, publications, and more.

To learn about volume discounts available if you order additional copies of this book, or about our any of our programs, please contact us today at:

LegalBizDev
225 Franklin St., 26th Floor
Boston, MA 02110
800-49-TRAIN
617-217-2578
Fax 917-386-2733
info@legalbizdev.com
www.legalbizdev.com